THE UNDETERMINED
DENIAL

ALBERT M. SWASH

authorHOUSE®

AuthorHouse™
1663 Liberty Drive
Bloomington, IN 47403
www.authorhouse.com
Phone: 1 (800) 839-8640

Published by AuthorHouse 06/11/2020

ISBN: 978-1-7283-6146-8 (sc)
ISBN: 978-1-7283-6144-4 (hc)
ISBN: 978-1-7283-6145-1 (e)

Library of Congress Control Number: 2020908491

CONTENTS

DEDICATION

To my dear wife Iris who dedicated 52 years to me

To my second wife Enid
Who passed away peacefully in 2017

To Mary Daniels
Who urged me to write this at a critical time in my life

To my very special friend Marie Spibey
Who thoughtfully named this project

Born February 17, 1922 in Chelmsford, Essex, England.

Graduated from Moulsham Street Elementary School in 1936 at the age of 14.

Volunteered for the Royal Marines in 1940. Served in North Africa. Met Iris Davies of Cromer following the war, and married her in Norwich, England in 1947.

Emigrated to Canada in 1954, where he enlisted with the Royal Canadian Corps of Signals in Kingston, Ontario 1954. Served in Egypt and Germany and was discharged in 1972. Employed as a civilian communications supervisor (Cryptographer) in the Halifax dockyard's 1972-84. Moved to British Columbia in 1984 where he lived at Cobble Hill, Ladysmith, on Vancouver Island. He now resides in Maple Ridge British Columbia.

CHAPTER 1

Black Monday

The room felt small and confining, the walls threatening, we had been asked to leave room 209, a number to be forever engraved on my mind. The recalcitrant nurse had at last understood the condition of my wife, and had finally visited the room, almost 4 hours after being informed that her patient was complaining of lack of oxygen. How could this be?

Within 10 minutes a "Code Blue" had been issued, and a team of doctors and nurses had descended, albeit, probably too late. I sat numbly on my chair, I could not believe, at this moment I was facing the possibility of being:

"Alone in the world."

My ignorance of the importance of oxygen would live with me for ever. My friends sat across the small room from me, the fear of the outcome so obvious, by the look on their faces.

We had pleaded for some attention from the nursing staff, only to be turned away, it appeared:

"As meddling relatives."

The sight of the oxygen meter with its low reading, had forewarned us of the impending panic. Our marriage had not been blessed with wealth, health is more important, and we had been fortunate enough to enjoy that until now.

We had travelled the world, climbed the mountains of love and good times, and also descended to the valleys of trials and tribulations, and survived the many pitfalls that can break some marriages.

Progeny had escaped us. Missing at this time for me, was the arm of a loving son or daughter around my shoulders to say:

"Everything will be alright dad." I had been truly blessed with the love of a wonderful woman, enjoyed the companionship of a truly caring person. She unfortunately had one fault, which will be described later, my love for her never wavered.

I heard footsteps coming down the hall, a nurse entered, looked across at me and said:

"Your wife would like to see you."

My friend took my hand, I could feel the love and understanding in her grasp, as we made our fearful way back to the room of impending destiny.

My life flashed in front of me...................

CHAPTER 2

The Meeting

We met in a rather amusing way, I had first seen her standing behind the counter of a Marks and Spencer outlet in Chelmsford, Essex, England. In fact, I had made it a daily habit to have my tea break morning and afternoon at their lunch bar. I did not realize it at the time, that I was wearing my Trilby hat at a rakish angle. I am certain that I was trying to copy Humphrey Bogart, the screen idol of the day, trying no doubt, to create an image of self-confidence.

Imagine my joy on entering a dance establishment the following Saturday night, to see my dream girl sitting on the side of the hall, with her girlfriend, no other man near her.

I had lacked the courage to ask her for a date in the store, but here was my chance.

Being quite a dandy on the dance floor, I engaged another girl to dance with me. It disturbed me somewhat, that both of them burst into hearty laughter each, and every time, I passed by their seats.

Uncharacteristic of my normal behavior of being shy with the fairer sex, whenever I requested them to dance with me, I set off across the hall, confronted her, and asked politely:

"Can we laugh this one out together?"

She rose slowly, put her arms up in the customary dancing position. I closed in, and the love of my life was in my arms. It mattered not that she trod all over my feet, or that she had not been dancing very long,

I was prepared to dance with her for as long as it took, I was truly smitten. Later I was to learn that the reason for the hearty laughter, was, that she had, named me "Slinky" (I immediately discarded the Trilby hat, it was obvious to me that she had noticed my daily interest in her.

There is an old adage which says:

"Love at first sight,"

Not so with her, she had experienced the fact that for a man to say:

"I love you,"

so quickly after meeting you, was just a line to get you in the back seat of the car, or some such place, so for her saying;

"I love you"

took much longer for her, and it had to be proven, in fact, it was difficult for her to say those words, even after 52 years of marriage.

We continued our courtship as lovers do. We had two separations, one early in our relationship, which came about as she thought I was getting too serious.

One night she informed me that she would not commit herself to any man, saying:

"I like you, but I am just not ready, I think it best if we do not see each other again."

I was disappointed beyond all reason, as in our very short association she had completely captured my heart.

The very next Saturday I arrived at the dance hall a little late, as I stood on the edge of the dance floor surveying all those present.

my eyes immediately caught sight of my dream girl dancing with a "Blue Job" (Air force type.)

I tried to act nonchalantly, forcing a smile, while at the same taking an instant dislike to her partner. Later in the evening, during the intermission, it was normal to congregate down the street at the local pub to imbibe in some alcoholic beverages.

It was there I found myself standing at the bar, just a few patrons away from Iris and her new beau. After a few minutes she tried hard not to acknowledge my presence, so I called out her:

"How about having a half pint with me for old times' sake?"

The glare I got from the RAF type, made my evening. Now he knew how I felt!

On re-entering the hall and taking advantage of the first excuse me dance, I pried her away from her partner, not just for that dance, but for the rest of the evening.

We were a couple again, for a short while at least. Later in our courtship I had arranged to play cricket one evening for a local club. I was certain that I had told her of this upcoming event. After the game, I rode my bicycle to where she was living, only to find out she had left some time earlier to go back to her home in Cromer, Norfolk, taking all her worldly belongings with her.

I took off to the railway station immediately to find out the time of the next train. No bags, and I had very little money left after I had paid the fare. I arrived in Norwich, where I had to change trains, only to find I was too late for the last connection to my destination. I still remember trying to get some sleep on the hard-wooden bench on the platform.

The next day I staked myself outside her house waiting for her to put in an appearance. Sometime later, she came out, sitting in the passenger side of her father's car, she noticed me straight away, but the car drove on, finally it did stop, she alighted, and walked back toward me, "To say she was not happy," would be putting mildly,

"Why have you come here?" she asked

"Simple," I replied,

"I am in love with you, and I do not want to give you up."

We walked along the promenade, then we sat on the sand discussing our future (or lack of it.) depending on who was doing the talking, four hours later we kissed and agreed that we would give it another try. She had made one stipulation however, and that was that I come to Norwich to live. I would have gone to Timbuktu if she had but asked me.

She obtained lodgings with a friend of the family, as for me, I was not so lucky. I had to go into lodgings for the first time in my life, this made me even more determined to get married.

One morning on coming down for breakfast (there were five of us at the table) I was greeted by the landlady telling me:

"There is no egg for you, your egg was bad."

That was the first time in my life I realized that hens laid eggs with names on.

The Betrayal

It took a year, but she finally realized that my intentions were indeed honorable. One other stipulation was that I get my divorce papers, fortunately, I had received my Divorce Nisi just three weeks before we were married in Norwich in 1947.

We spent a short honeymoon at Westcliffe–on–Sea in Essex, where, just a few years previous, in the same hotel, I had been billeted with the Royal Marines. What a coincidence! We found a one room apartment with kitchen privileges, and we were so happy to be together, neither of us realized that marriage is just not always that easy.

We had six years of early problems, including three moves. Our life in a one-room flat was too restrictive. One day my wife saw an advertisement in the paper for help in a large house in the country, in return for a small stipend. This of course came with accommodation. My wife was to prepare meals and serve dinner at night. She was interested.

Having spent the pre-war years in service in a large house for the gentry, she was fully aware of the demands of the position. She convinced me to make the change. It turned out we were working for an egotistical retired Army Colonel with an alcoholic wife, this was a lesson in life of its own. This worked out well for a year and gave us an opportunity to put a little money into a Building Society, which led to us later purchasing our first home.

What a mansion it was, when judged by the scale of living in North America, a three-floor brick monstrosity, which came complete with an "Outside John," which was dry, and had to be emptied regularly. We got our water from a pump, shared with our neighbour in the adjoining backyard. There was a brick copper in the corner of the kitchen fuelled by coal for boiling the weekly wash, it had a coal fireplace which had to heat the whole house. How often have we sat listening to the radio, scorched in the front, while our backs were icy cold? We always had chilblains on our feet. For long years we stayed in this romantic hideaway, keeping four pigs in the backyard to try and make an extra pound (Buck) digging a half acre with a spade to plant and reap potatoes, to feed us, and the pigs. Another use for the brick copper, was to boil tasty potato and bran mash, for the animals of course. We commuted to work daily, 6 miles each way in all weathers, on a (put- put) bicycle. I did the pedaling with Iris on the cross bar. For the uninitiated, a Put-Put bicycle had a small motor, which ran off of the side of the back tire.

However, life and love were wonderful with one exception we had not been blessed with progeny. My wife was getting anxious. She talked me into going with her to see a doctor and find out why all our life and love and not been suitably rewarded.

This led to tests and one of the most embarrassing times of my life. The doctor told me to report to the hospital to a special department, which turned out to be a long room with dozens of lab technicians, mostly female. A nurse gave me a little jar, pointed to the men's room at the far end of the room, and said:

"You know what I want"

"A urine sample," I replied.

"No" she said

"A sperm sample."

I shuffled by the crowd of smiling, and knowing faces., to carry out my task. What happened to that old theory?

"You will go blind if you do that," I thought.

Gingerly replacing the cap on the jar, I opened the door, at the same time trying carefully to keep my sample covered, and, blushing like a new bride, I returned to the nurse with my trophy.

All of this had no effect on the manufacture of a little one, and the doctors only advice was to keep on trying, just as if I needed any excuse to do that.

The first blip in our happy marriage came soon after. My wife took a day off from work, I returned home early that afternoon to an empty house.

As this was unusual, I thought that my wife had maybe taken a walk, so I drove around the village. I was very disturbed when I came around a corner to see my wife arm in arm with another man. I confronted them and told my wife to get in the car.

After arriving home, I made it very clear that this had happened to me once before in my former marriage, and that I did not intend it to happen again. She made frantic efforts, with lots of apologies, accompanied by tears, but I was not taken in with this. My heart was broken, I did not think this would ever happen, she pointed everything seemed to be going so well. But betrayal is very difficult to forgive. What made it even more difficult to accept, was that he was my best friend.

Life was very difficult for several weeks after that, making it even worse is when you have an erring wife sitting on the cross-bar inches away from your face, and knowing you will never trust her again.

Life for both of us was about to take a drastic change, one that we had not expected or planned for. Suddenly, from out of the blue we decided to give up this life with its many disadvantages and crossed, the sea to Canada.

The Journey

March 4, 1954 dawned sunny and bright as our train filled with immigrants and others, all bent on a more pleasurable reason for visiting the new country than I. We drew into the Liverpool docks alongside this enormous black hulk bearing the name R.M.S. Ascania, we proceeded up the gangplank to enter this huge cavern of luxury.

It was like entering a palace, the decor and fittings were so majestic, all this added to the excitement of this memorable event in our young lives. We were escorted to our cabin, this was not on the grand scale of the rest of the ship, small but comfortable, if somewhat cramped. Shortly thereafter, we were conscious of the steady pulse of the engines, with the accompanying vibration felt throughout the great vessel. Our great adventure was taking one more step.

We proceeded down the Irish Sea on one of those rare days that it was not showing its angry self, so we enjoyed a warm sunny afternoon, gazing at the coastline, as our Mother country slipped past. We entered Cobh Harbor in South Ireland to take on more passengers from a launch, precariously loading humans and cargo up the gangway.

"Lunch is served"

Was relayed over the loud speaker system, as we made our way to the main dining room. At this juncture, I must point out that my lady love, although coming from a fishing family on the East Coast, was most apprehensive at the thought of crossing the Atlantic Ocean.

We were enjoying a most beautiful meal, served in the lap of luxury, as was so truly advertised by the Cunard company.

This turned out to be the last meal for my wife, as she unfortunately, proceeded shortly thereafter to survive on Dry Ginger ale and dry biscuits, for the whole journey. I had noticed while dining, the crew were quietly, but efficiently closing the portholes and chaining the tables to the floor.

I realized immediately that we were about to up anchor and sail into rough seas. Not wanting to upset my partner, I kept this observation to myself, allowing her to enjoy to the full this splendid repast.

Once again, the engines started, and we sailed out of Cobh Harbor into the Atlantic. We had no sooner crossed the bar, when this huge monster began to rise and fall, with the sound of the angry ocean slapping the bows.

This was the start of five days of seasickness, which lasted until Iris finally escaped the cabin, when, much lighter in weight, and color, she was able to come on deck for the second time, as we sailed close to Newfoundland. Just one day out from our destination, Halifax, Nova Scotia.

This enabled her to be in time to see a remarkable event off of the Grand Banks. I knew from reading articles that this was one of the most proficient fishing areas in the whole world.

The surprising thing to me was the way the harvesting of the fish was carried out. Here, seemingly in the middle of the Atlantic

Ocean, were small "Dories" separated from their mother vessels, blithely carrying on their business of catching Cod. Was this the:

"Squid Jigging Ground" from the famous Newfie sea Shanty.

You might be wondering at this moment if I still remember how things were between us. They were not the same, and as I feel at this moment, they never will be completely.

CHAPTER 5

The Arrival

Our destination in the promised land was Cole harbour just a few miles east of Dartmouth, Nova Scotia. The intention of us coming here was that we were to work on the poultry farm of Iris's brother, eventually coming to be joint owners. However, it soon became obvious that this was not the intention of the in-law. We were subjected to a life completely foreign to us. My wife spent long hours in the egg washing department, in a damp humid environment It was not long before she was ill with Rheumatic Fever – the relations called it homesickness.

I spent my time collecting eggs and feeding the fowl, in a foul atmosphere.

Is it any wonder that I have an aversion for chicken in any way shape or form to this day? we were completely out of our medium.

After collecting several millions of these oval wonders, I never did find one with my name on it. Four months of bitterness and disappointment, led to an unpleasant and long-standing separation. We were dropped off at the Dartmouth ferry with our meagre belongings.

We had to find accommodation and work in a strange city, this setback did not force us to give up on Canada, more importantly, or on our marriage. We "sucked it in" as they say in Canada, and went back to a one room apartment.

Finding work was not easy for me, and I had to settle for a job in a hardware company, which sold to independent outlets throughout the province. the hours were long and the pay short, and it was not long before they used my previous experience to reorganize their premises. $35 did not go far in those days.

Iris on the other hand, was more fortunate as she landed a position with the Robert Simpson company, coincidentally as a stockroom clerk. She soon fitted in, and was very happy in her work, and was given added responsibilities which eventually led to her holding a buyer position for the cosmetic department. We moved into a nicer apartment, but this was still below the standard of living we had become accustomed to.

There are many English terms that mean quite the opposite here in Canada, as my wife was soon to learn. When she looked back on it, it was quite humorous. She was engaged in a conversation with a fellow member at lunch one day, the friend was explaining to my wife, that her brother was the manager of a large super store and that his wife was a French Canadian. My wife casually remarked that the brother must get a good screw. Her companion was very put out with this and made it clear to the manager, that she did not want to work with my wife anymore.

Fortunately for her, the manager had served with the Canadian Air Force during the war in Britain, so he explained to her that what Iris meant was:

"I bet he gets a good wage."

All's well that ends well, but she did not make that mistake again. While being frustrated with my current position, we came in contact with a young couple, of whom the man was a Captain in the Royal Canadian Engineers. What began as conversations about the war and my military experiences led to him suggesting that I would make much more money, and at the same time improve our standard of living, if I joined the Canadian Army.

I had volunteered for the Royal Marines, and had served until the end of the war. On demobilization, however, I had decided that was a sufficient length of time for me of army life.

We talked over my proposed enlistment very carefully. The medical and educational tests were just a formality, and in mere days I was swearing allegiance to her Majesty the Queen, and qualifying for my first pay parade.

Of course, my better half was not happy at the thought of me having to be away on basic training for nine months, especially as the plan included me going to Chilliwack in British Columbia, or, failing that, to my second choice, the Royal Canadian Corps of Signals in Kingston, Ontario.

I have a strong feeling that life is planned out, regardless of what one might want to wish for. I am a convinced fatalist, and knew in my heart that some how things will turn out for me.

So, I found myself kissing my dear Iris goodbye for the first time that called for a long separation between us.

I boarded the train to Kingston; my first choice of Chilliwack having been ruled out that the very last moment. As I said, this was my first disconnection from Iris, and although I did not recognize it at the time, sitting in the train speeding away from my love, peace for me would soon be shattered.

CHAPTER 6

The Parting and the Promotion

As we clung together on Halifax Station to say our farewells, I noticed some misting in her eyes, a tremor in her voice and trembling in her body. I had to keep saying to myself:

"Grown men don't cry."

It was a lasting memory, as poignant to me now as it was so long ago. The military rules state, that we would not be together again until I received my first posting in nine months, it was almost like receiving a life sentence.

The Loud hailer called out:

"All those recruits going to Montréal gather at the loading gate."

I took my last kiss, and proceeded to take the next step in my life. Realizing that I had to be trusting that all would be well while I was away.

I joined in the rabble – they could hardly be called less – gathering at the gate, all of them, except me, with pink cheeks, the bum fluff still evident on their boyish features. Then along came this cocky little Officer who had inherited his first "Pip" (2Lt) the previous day, and unknowingly, he got us on the second.

He managed to get us lined up, and looked us over, I had nicknamed him in my mind as:

"Field Marshall Montgomery" he was that pompous.

"Swash" he yelled:

"Hear sir" I replied

"Get out here." he continued

He then addressed the squad, for want of a better name:

"This is Swash"

he went on:

"He is my representative, I will tell him what I want, and you will do what he tells you to do."

This trip was a nightmare, those kids, wild and let out of the cage for the first time, would have destroyed everything they came in contact with, if they had been left to run free. I was not allowed time to reflect on my recent parting, my time was completely taken up getting them out of one scrape after another, while Monty enjoyed the peace and quiet of his sleeping car.

My biggest embarrassment came on the railway station at Rimouski in Northern Québec. My pretentious officer had informed me that we would be stopping here for forty minutes:

"I want you to march them up and down the platform for twenty-five minutes" he said.

After I managed to get all eighteen of them out on the platform, I formed them up in three rows. The use of the proper orders, would only have added more confusion.

"What now?" I asked myself.

This crew had received no military training, consequently, they knew no orders for marching or stopping. This left me facing a quandary.

To the crowded patrons of Canadian National gathered waiting for the train's departure, we must have looked like a segment out of the Sgt Bilco sitcom. I found myself replacing Left Turn with Turn that way, Quick March with Start Walking and Halt with Stop, it was a riot, but one I wanted to forget in a hurry.

Eventually we arrived in Montréal where I gave up my baby-sitting job, changed trains, and proceeded to Kingston, Ontario. The future Field Marshal (In his eyes at least, did tell me I had done a good job, and he would make sure that my commanding officer would be informed of my potential.

Knowing how much influence that would carry in my coming environment, I did not attempt to pin my stripes on right away. You will find out in the next chapter his reference of my ability, did not precede me to Vimy Barracks.

Leaving Montréal for Kingston, gave me time for more thought of my wife and just how much she meant to me, I just know she would not have laughed, as so many did on the station, she was too understanding for that.

But some doubts of her possible behaviour remained in my mind.

CHAPTER 7

More Military Woes

If I had thought my inception into the Canadian Army might be a nightmare, I was about to find out that I had a lot to learn. My previous forty-eight hours had just been a drop in the bucket. Arriving in Kingston at 1:30 AM, I was expecting transport to the barracks - how wrong could I be – the platform was bare, no welcoming committee from the camp. I found the nearest telephone box, and managed to find the number of the barracks from the badly mutilated telephone directory

"Will you send transport for me." I asked:

The answer could not have been curter:

"Get a taxi"

Eventually arriving in the guard house where the Sgt. greeted me with the following comment:

"We have a room for incoming recruits, but as it is so late now, you can sleep in one of the cells."

This turned out to be a solid wooden frame six inches above floor level, the wind whistled through the door, and under my bed. He gave me one blanket, so I laid down to contemplate my life so far as a soldier, I had been promoted and put in the jailhouse in just two days.

"Obviously the biggest mistake of my life, best sums it up."

Six o'clock in the morning the friendly sergeant woke me up, showed me the washroom, thus enabling me to carry out my ablutions. He then gave me a member of the guard to show me to the mess hall. I must admit, this was the first good thing that I had experienced. The bacon and eggs, and the coffee were delicious.

It soon became apparent that this was the day the Commanding Officer did his inspection; I remember it still as "Black Friday." I was shown where number one squadron headquarters was situated.

This was the recruit training section for the School of Signals. I then proceeded to report into camp. Opening the door, I was immediately met with this character doing drill all by himself in front of a full-length mirror, he was The Company Sergeant Major. I am sure his demise has been prayed for many times, as he was feared by all and sundry, his first words to me were:

"Get a haircut." he followed that up by yelling:

"Get lost until the CO's inspection has finished."

By now my conviction of having made the biggest mistake of my life was solidified, but I was now powerless to change it.

The events that followed are unbelievable but nevertheless true. Since I had last passed the parade square, four Sgts, complete with drill sticks, were manning each of the four corners.

I was walking with my little bag trying to carry out my orders to get lost, when a loud stentorian voice yelled:

"Get your head up, swing those G---- D---- arms." he couldn't mean me I thought:

"You with the little bag, get over here, you miserable little man." He went on.

Again, I thought it cannot be me I'm over six feet tall, but I went over anyway. Obviously, I was the butt of his wrath. He proceeded to tell me my life's history, or at least the part about my coming into the world, this was news to me, as I was certain my parents were legally married. If you get my drift.

After surviving his five-minute tirade and having him show me the correct height to swing my arms, he released me to continue getting lost. Remembering being told that I had to have a haircut, this despite having one the day before I left Halifax.

Oh! I thought, this would be an ideal place to kill some time, so I made my next port of call the barbershop. Gus, a civilian, born in the Ukraine, hastily told me he did not have much time as he was also preparing for the Commanding Officers inspection. Very soon thereafter, it was to my discovery, that Gus had not had a course in barbering, for, in about two minutes my:

"Short back and sides," had become a "Yul Brenner."

Emerging from his two-minute shearing, I saw a sign pointing to the canteen. I decided this might be the place to sojourn for a few more time-wasting minutes from marching round and round the camp, still trying to get lost.

"A coffee and doughnut please" I asked the rotund, but pleasant cashier.

I paid her, and retreated to a table up against the wall, as by now I was trying desperately not to have anyone behind me who would further insult my entry into this world. I had barely had time to sip my coffee, when a group of men in blue coveralls, mops and pails, strode into the canteen. A Cpl asked me:

"What are you doing here"

Before I could even reply, he yelled:

"Get lost"

This had to be the slogan of this camp, if so, I was learning it fast.

My final humiliation of the day came just before eleven o'clock, when I was in the wrong place at the wrong time, when I encountered the aforementioned Commanding Officer, and his entourage. I was, marching along with my arms up high, when I should have stopped and faced this personage of such great power in the military.

He passed by me with nary a glance, but the camp Regimental Sergeant Major was not so charitable. Once again, I heard those menacing words:

"Get over here," and once again I was subjected to another tongue lashing, this time however, he did not bring my parents into it.

Thank goodness lunch time finally arrived, although all of the preceding developments in the morning had left me far from being hungry, my problems were still not behind me. Carrying my tray along the serving line, the cook offered me cream corn, and thinking I was being funny, I quipped:

"We feed chickens with that where I came from."

Then the next cook in line, was the mash potato man, and I received more on my suit than I did on my plate. I retreated to lick my wounds of that memorable morning, which still sticks vividly in my mind to this day.

CHAPTER 8

Basic Misery to Ecstasy

It was Sunday, and the second day of my new life, not like the holy day that I had got to love so much at home, a day when we were together alone, to partake in what ever pursuits made the other partner happy. Today I was surrounded by eager recruits spitting and polishing their equipment, some of whose boots shone bright enough to show their reflection. Blanco, a drab coloured liquid which was a covering for the web components of a soldier's equipment, this had been applied where necessary.

The age difference had already taken an affect, my comrades tended to congregate among themselves, rather than associate with me, I must have seemed so old to these mere lads.

I had one big advantage however, as I had spoken home for a few brief minutes on the telephone, far be it for me to worry about her with the misery I had so far received in my new career, I left her upbeat and happy, if only I felt the same way here. Promises were made by us, that the next few months would pass quickly, and we could renew our lives together.

As it happened I was the last recruit to join the 30-man squad, some of whom had been there three weeks and their gear was pretty well up to shape, as for the rest of us, we were all at the stage where we had just received our kit, this left me at the back of the pack, as mine was still in the quartermaster's store.

I did not fall asleep very fitfully that night, so when I entered the quartermasters store the next morning to be kitted out, my attitude was not conducive to the further indignities I was exposed to. I think they called it "new recruit abuse"

This passed off as making a man of you.

One of the things issued to me, which at the time, I did not attach much importance to, were my medal ribbons from world War II. Army tradition requires that if you have any decorations you must wear them on your uniform, this also includes recruits. These ribbons were to cause me a lot of trouble, as later entries will reveal.

First day on parade came, and I was introduced to my Sergeant and my Corporal for the next six months, they both were a good six or seven years younger than I was, with no medal ribbons on their chests.

The sight of mine, I believe, was the start of my problems, as I soon found out that my Sgt. Maj along with these other two morons, were extremely high on EGO, but very low on IQ.

It appeared that my decorations challenged their normal sadistic behaviour, and their approach to it was to give me a hard time. A fellow recruit, while not a recruit as such, had changed from the Corps of Military Police, so he soon became my ally, and fellow scapegoat.

It was not long before the Sgt always referred to me as:

"Grand Dad.

So, it gave me great pleasure this one time, although at the time it caused me great pain. My Sgt had marched us into the gymnasium, and turned us over to the Physical Training Instructor, and before he left, he asked:

"What are you doing this morning?"

The PTI pointed to the horse, a 6 or 7-foot-long padded bench about 4 feet above the ground, "Oh" chortled my Sgt. "I must stay and watch Grand Dad do this."

We then circled the gymnasium to pick up enough momentum for the jump, I was almost at the end of the line, watching one after another of these young blood's make pitiful attempts at clearing this hurdle. Determined in my own mind to make the Sgt feel stupid, I built up my determination to do it or bust.

Suffice to say, I sprang off the board, stretched my arms as far forward as I could, pulled my legs up behind me. I cleared it cleanly, but for my tailbone, which just caught the end of the horse. The pain was excruciating, and tears were very close to showing, but I smiled, and was rewarded by the following remark by the PTI:

"Sgt. Green it is a pity you do not have 29 other Grand Dads in your squad," revenge was mine, sweet revenge.

Let me proceed to the midpoint of this nine months of hell, and get closer to the reunion that I longed for so much. We had a midcourse kit inspection, which, if we passed, would allow us to go into Kingston at the weekends.

Immediately my brain started working, why not get Iris up here, even if I could only see her at the weekends.

It was against the rules, but what the heck, who would know.? It would mean that I would have to pay for the costs of getting her to Kingston, but that would not be a problem. Would she come? Only one way to find out, ask her. She told me on the telephone that:

"Wild horses would not keep her away, when can I come" she replied "I am so unhappy away from you"

The first weekend I was free, I found a bedsitter, paid the rent for the month, raced to the nearest telephone booth and passed on the good news.

"Have you any idea when you can come" I asked

"It must be at the weekend, if I am to meet you," I continued

"How about two weekends from now" she answered

I could just feel the excitement in her voice.

"You make the train inquiries, I told her, and I will ring next Saturday."

I hardly noticed the abuse the next two weeks, I am sure the instructors were confused by my change of attitude, try as they might, they would not get under my skin now.

Patiently waiting for the train, it just seemed the norm for me these days, it was two hours late. She finally stepped down from the train, she was wearing something I had never seen before and my heart exploded, how I love that lovely lady. We embraced for a few minutes, I was in another world, Kingston from the place I hated so much, had just lit up like a neon sign

CHAPTER 9

Food Love and Other Things

There are things in one's life that remain in your memory forever, like the hit tune on our honeymoon "Oklahoma" and another was the overwhelming joy I was experiencing on this day. Iris was dressed in a salmon coloured suit, hemline provocatively placed just above the knee, a filmy white blouse, flesh coloured nylons, with white shoes and handbag.

I was so proud of her; I was so lucky to call her my own. I still could not see what she had ever seen in me, but oh so grateful that she had. Proudly escorting her out of the station to the waiting taxi, short on cash, but not on class, nothing but the best was in order this day, I led her to the cab, holding hands and stealing a kiss, I called out to the cabbie:

"Take us to the best restaurant in town driver."

We eventually arrived at the restaurant, where we dined on the best T-bone steak in the house. When I told her how nice she looked, she said:

"I kept it on a hanger until I was near, as I wanted to look my very best for you," her lovely eyes glowed as she said it.

Finally arriving at our rather less-than-luxurious apartment, we settled into unpacking what small amount she had been able to carry.

We had partaken of the food, how could love be far away. The day was still young, but who was looking at the clock! Humor, they say makes your day, our reunion fell in that category. Here we were, back in a small apartment, (Would we ever escape to a better abode.) this one had previously been linked to Queens University students, who it seems, must have used the bed for a trampoline or some similar activity. Our first occupation of it caused it to collapse, as the brick, which had been supplanted to replace the leg, could not stand the activity. As the song says:

"We got right up and started all over again."

Having no television or radio, caused us little hardship, we had lots to talk about, both past and for the future. I kept the misery of my daily life from her, telling her a little white lie that everything was fine, no need to upset her. I explained that I could not get home from Monday to Friday, as I was supposed to be back in barracks on Saturday night.

Throwing conformity to the winds, I did not go back on that Saturday night, fortunately for me, there was no bed check on the following Sunday morning, and I found out:

"Never on Sunday" as the film said.

So, unless I catch a duty, I had my weekends with her. However, I had to take stuff home to clean otherwise I would not be ready for the Monday morning parade, this way I had someone to help me:

"What would my Sgt. think?"

We were so full from lunch we never required tea, so we went out and had a look downtown, visited the local movie house, most things I can remember, but not the name of the movie. Stopping at a coffee house on the way home we sipped and giggled like newlyweds, which was exactly how we felt.

Sunday was spent enjoying each other's company until I had to get the bus back to barracks and the reality of my other life.

CHAPTER 10

Return to Barrack Blues

When you enter Vimy barracks, you are greeted by a statue of Mercury, the mythical god of speed. I should remember the motto that accompanies this, but it escapes me. We, however, had given it its own designation, "Abandon hope all ye who enter here." He, like all great Roman statues, was made prominent by huge protuberances. One graduation squad had made Corps history by painting it white. If our group decided on some such vengeance, my proposition would have been to cut it off completely, he deserves no enjoyment in life for what went on behind these walls.

This particular Monday morning was different, my change of attitude must have been significantly altered, and visible, causing my sergeant to remark:

"You look happy this morning Granddad," you must have had a good weekend."

"Yes sir" I replied.

Chalk up two more brownie points for me at his expense. He didn't know the half of it:

"I will soon change that," he said, but that was something beyond his power.

The day- to-day torture now became more bearable, whenever we had tests on weapons and other various aspects of our training, I had very little difficulty topping my comrades, this was something the NCO' S could not change.

Nearing the end of my basic training I finally got my chance to rock the infamous Sgt. on his heels.

We were engaged with two other squads out in the field for five days roughing it, and doing field exercises. During my years as a Royal Marine, I had been a member of the M.N.B.D.O (Mobile Naval Base Defence Organization.)

Our purpose was to land in a port city when our forces were being driven back, and defend it for as long as possible, ports being the lifeline of any Army. Tobruk in north Africa was a splendid example of this, as when Field Marshall Rommel, (German army) drove the allies back to Al Alamein in Egypt, he never did take Tobruk.

. The Sgt. for some reason had seen something funny in the letters MNBDO, and took great personal satisfaction at singing it out whenever he could, this was an attempt to rile me up, putting myself into a position, where he could have me put into detention for insubordination.

One day at lunch time, while we were on exercises, we were sitting on our butts eating stew from a mess can, when three sergeants, appeared to brief us for the afternoon tasks.

My Sgt. could not resist the temptation to show off in front of his compatriots by suggesting that the honourable Mr. MNBDO might give them his war experience, and tell all and sundry how it should be done. He got his usual laugh from his captive audience, he also succeeded in finally getting to me. I had simply had enough, and rose to his bait.

Standing up to attention, and being military in my actions, I said:

31

"Excuse me Sgt.," the MNBDO seems to be very funny to you. I would like to inform you that to many of my comrades who are still there with tiny white crosses above their graves in the sand, it is far from being funny".

I thought he was going to have apoplexy, his face went red, he then stomped toward me, and had to be restrained by his fellow NCOs.

He called for two of our squad to come forward to escort me to the truck, to take me back to the camp guard room. However, calmer minds stepped in and the other sergeants took him on one side, and they must have explained to him that he had overstepped the line.

They then came over to me, informed the escorts that they were no longer required, and I was released to my own cognizant. Three strikes to me, and from then on to our graduation I received very little attention from him.

On re-entering a normal existence on the Sunday, I refrained from telling Iris of my confrontation, as she had continually told me to keep my cool and ride it out.

What a joy it was to be free of the regimental side of my life and re-enter the loving relationship of our marriage. We crammed every minute of our time together. Our trips were confined to the shores of Lake Ontario, as we had no source of transportation to venture further afield. Sunday night came too fast, but the greater part of the nine months was behind us.

CHAPTER 11

Coincidence

With only ten more days to go until my graduation, the following Sunday morning felt really great to me, but I could not understand why my partner was so quiet, as we prepared our breakfast together.

We sat down to eat and she looked hard at me, saying:

"Have you anything to tell me?" I was at a complete loss for words, as the source of her question puzzled me:

"No," I replied:

"Should I."

We had been staying in this penthouse lodgings for two months now, and on each Saturday evening our landlord and his wife had dressed up in their finery to go out for the evening.

They had arranged for us to babysit their young children, giving us the chance to watch some TV, which was still quite a novelty, plus we made a few valuable dollars.

Unbeknown to us, their destination was the Sgt.'s Mess in Vimy, where they were Honorary Members, and very well respected. In fact, "Stan the man" (the private nickname for the aforementioned Sgt. Major,) being a personal friend.

The topic of conversation on this particular night was regarding a recruit who had challenged one of their own, with a verbal rebuttal, during the previous week's training.

My name had been divulged, and the story was picked up by our landlord and his wife. This left her eagerly awaiting the chance to pass it on. Unfortunately for me, the lady of the house was so anxious to divulge this tidbit, she told Iris immediately on returning from the mess.

"You got your self in trouble last week, why did you not tell me?" she asked:

Simple" I replied, "I did not want to upset you."

She gave me a hard-penetrating look and snapped:

"How do I know you have not held anything else from me, I am not amused?"

This was obviously the time to open up and tell her of the trials and tribulations that I had tried to hide from her. We mended our fences in short order, a trend that we were able to do on most occasions, and the temporary blip was just that, a blip.

This was not to be my day, for later in the evening, during a nice meal in a restaurant, who should walk in but Cpl. Parton the other half of my training team. He sat down at a table facing us with his lady friend, or wife, I had never been interested in their marital status.

Looking over at us, he made no sign of recognition, which neither disturbed or bothered me. I sensed however, that this was not the last I would hear of it. True to form, at the first opportunity on Monday morning, in front of our squad, while we were on parade he yelled:

"I saw you with your Mother on Sunday, Swash".

My patience and temper had taken a lot of abuse over the past six months, and I still do not know to this day, how I controlled myself, this was the ultimate insult. I registered his name in my mental notebook, I would get this SOB sometime down the line, he had just made himself my personal enemy.

Graduation came and went, we had the usual graduation party, where everyone was supposed to kiss and make up, and the sadists informed us it was just to make us into men.

From then on, I had only three months left for my trade training. For me it would be in teletype communications, which I had requested, and I hoped for a fresh start. We would still remain in Vimy, but just move into new quarters.

We had the Thursday to move out of there, and into a new barrack block. On the completion this procedure, we had the rest of the day off plus, the Friday, to make it a long weekend.

The weather was great, Iris and I had discovered that we could get a bus to Ganonoque, which was the gateway to the Thousand Islands. We celebrated with two days in a motel, our first endeavor of that experience, but not our last.

Often since, I have heard that for the best way to repair a broken marriage, you should check into a motel with very little baggage.

While this was not the case with us, it does seem to create an atmosphere for good results. Doing anything with her was always a delight, and to please her was my ultimate aim at all times. This little town remains a treasure in my memory, little did I know at the time, it would play a big part in my future. I had put the bad episode of the betrayal, in the back of my mind, while at the same time trying desperately to think it never ever happened.

CHAPTER 12

My Other Half

Everyone is aware that it takes two to tango, it is equally true that It takes two to make a successful marriage. At this point in my story I will introduce my other half, Iris.

Born in 1921 on the East Coast of England in a small seaside place called Cromer. Her father was a crab fisherman, later to be promoted to become a Fisheries Officer. For many years he had been the engineer on the famous Cromer lifeboat, coxswained by the renowned, in England, Coxswain Blogg, and they both had been decorated several times for bravery, once by the King of Holland.

Her mother was the typical housewife of that day. They were brought up in a strict belief of the Plymouth brethren. Although not a practising member from her teens on, this grounding remained with her throughout her whole life. She was educated in the same small town, and on leaving school, tried her hand at a few local positions. On one occasion, she informed her superior that:

"If you do not like the way I am doing the job, you should get someone else". Moments later she was looking for another job. Those reading this story so far, who knew her, will readily identify those words with Iris.

During her upbringing, her father, who was the typical male member of the household, continually making demands on her mother. This strengthened a spirit in my wife that, no man would subject her to be a slave. I was told at the earliest possible minute:

"Never try anything like that on me."

For the next 52 years, anything that slightly resembled an order was quickly ignored, I learned fast that to:

"Suggest, to her, was the only way to go."

I digress, less than a year trying to cope with living in this small town, she decided to join her older sister in service as a "housemaid" with a well-known pottery family, and also coal, in the Midlands. I could fill a book of some of the things she did, and was accused of doing. At the age of 15 she was a teenage rebel. Unfortunately, this was where she learned her one bad habit. More on that later.

Every summer the Oakes's family moved North to Skipness Castle in Scotland. Iris was very happy there, and always wanted at some time to return to it, and take me with her. In 1988, we did just that, where we met Mrs. Oakes, now an elderly matron who still remembered my wife from all that time ago, she was obviously thrilled at meeting her again.

With the 1939-45 war on, Iris was not satisfied until she joined the WRAF (Woman's Royal Air Force Auxiliary) where she became a Radar operator, on the North-East coast of England. She served until the end of the war, and got an early discharge, as her mother was seriously ill.

As soon as her mother recovered, she was restless again, and decided to try to find employment in Chelmsford, Essex. Our lives were full of coincidences, and here was yet another one. In WW I her mother lived in Chelmsford, and as her father had been seriously injured, he was sent there from Cromer to recuperate.

ALBERT M. SWASH

They met, and subsequently were married. As Chelmsford was my hometown, Iris came the same route, we met, and the rest is history

I thank the Lord, for sending her and including me in his plans.

CHAPTER 13

A New Beginning

On the day of commencing my trades training, the apprehension of my reception in the classroom, was high on my mind. I decided that my first impression must be better than it had appeared to be, on my introduction to basic training. Iris had added to this feeling at our parting that morning, by telling me to:

"Try and be more approachable, and less belligerent."

"What on earth did she mean by that."

The classroom was set out with a Teletype machine for each student, plus a desk for the academic portions of the course. I noticed that a student's name had been assigned to each position, and we were told to find our place and sit down. While we waited for our instructors to enter the classroom, I remembered my last instructions from home, and made sure I had a smile on my face, and not a belligerent look on my countenance. Shortly after that, our class officer entered the room, followed by the Sgt. and the course Cpl., both of whom looked all right at this time, although I knew, only time would tell. The 2Lt read us the "Official Secrets Act, which I am subject to, to this day.

On his departure, the instructor gave us his official welcome, so far so good. "Now" he said, "I am going to call your name to enable me to put a face to that name."

Alphabetically I was near the last to be called, and everything was still going along fine. I began to feel a lot better:

"Swash" he called out:

"Sir" I replied.

He gave me a long hard look, here it comes, I thought.

"You are the guy who caused so much aggravation on your basic training, that is the reason I put your desk at the front and centre, so I can keep an eye on you, he paused for a second, then smiled and said:

"This is a fresh start for you, you will be treated like all of your classmates, it is up to you prove your self"

It had taken me six months to find a sergeant who had an IQ to match his ego. A few days later, more good news followed, at the end of classes one day, the instructor told me to remain behind. Closing the door, he said:

"So, I hear you have your wife in Kingston, I will try and get you an overnight pass."

A few days later I received permission to do just that, and the Army didn't seem so bad after all.

While I was getting established in my career, my better half was out, hitting the bricks, to find employment for herself. She was having little success, as Kingston, having two large military establishments, plus the Royal Military College, provided many wives to be available on the job market.

The first placement was not exactly what her Plymouth Brethren upbringing would recommend, she had found herself on the counter of the London Wine Store on Princess Street. She was very upset the first day, it seemed that fifty percent of her customers were brown baggers, that hang out in the back alleys and on the benches by Lake Ontario:

"You must quit, it is not worth the small amount of money you are making," I told her.

She gave it a few more days, and was thrilled when she answered an advertisement in the local grocery store outlet, where she was hired as a cashier. Now we had two contented members in the family.

One night while sitting in our apartment, my wife was looking through the for-sale section of the local newspaper. Excitedly she called out:

"Here is a bargain, we are making enough money to make a down payment, and it would be great for us to have."

She passed the advertisement over to me:

"What on earth are you talking about," I said, "We cannot afford a car."

"Yes, but look at the price," she answered, the advertisement said:

"For Sale" "1949 Ford Anglia in good condition one hundred dollars, and it is only five years old." she went on:

"We do not have one hundred dollars," I said,

"We can borrow it from a finance company, it won't take long to pay it off." was her reply. Her excitement was almost contagious.

"At least, let's go and have a look at it." was her instant reply.

I rose like a trout after a fly, how could I not at least please her by going out and having a look. The name painted on the side, should have been enough, "Fartin Jenny the Second."

The steering wheel was on the wrong side, and that should have said it all. "Take it for a ride." the owner said, did this woman know how to handle me!

We went around the block and it did feel good I must admit. The owner had brought the car over from England, and then found out he had to drive on the opposite side of the road over here.

I told him we would get back to him, so he took my telephone number, and he was ringing before we had settled back in our apartment:

"Oh, just a minute," she covered the phone with her hand:

"Albert, he has another man there that wants it," she begged, but we have the first chance, she went on.

It was a mistake, it turned out to be a proper fiasco, but do you know what, on looking back, I am glad I did, the love of my life enjoyed every hectic trip we made in Jenny. Wasn't making your spouse happy, what it is all about.?

CHAPTER 14

Small Mercies and Big Gains

Over my many years of life's experiences, two of those realizations are of major importance to me, and they remain that way to this day. The first of which is people who have money, and are able to buy anything their heart desires, do not receive the enjoyment of those, who have to scrimp and save for those special days.

For instance, would Bill Gates, the richest man in the world, really be thrilled to share an ice cream cone with his wife, I think not. His thrill would be that he could buy the vendor out. The second is fate, this came later in my life, but I am a confirmed fatalist. I will refer to that more at a later date.

The first of the above perceptions was born at this time. My wife was happy in her work, while I was enjoying to the limit my course on communications, we had a roof over our heads, and now we had wheels. What more could anyone ask for.?

We planned our first adventure in Jenny, the Saturday following her purchase, now that she had become our very own. This had not been easy, as we could not obtain financing in Kingston.

The owner, so anxious to get rid of his right-handed liability, and having found two suckers to take it over, drove us 75 miles to Belleville, where he was convinced that a loan could be made.

Smart man, he did not use the Anglia for this trip, but he rather proudly showed off its replacement. The deal was struck.

As the Saturday dawned, we arose early, as our destination for the day was the city of Ottawa one hundred miles as the crow flies. Iris had packed lunch, and a flask of tea, the thermos being provided by our friendly landlady.

Excitedly, she had informed her that we were thinking of going to Ottawa, Iris, was visibly disappointed at the lack of enthusiasm that was returned by the landlady.

We set out, and by the time we reached the first incline of any measure, we discovered where Jenny had got her name. The backfiring, and suggestive noises omitted by our tailpipe, would have been embarrassing, had it not been overshadowed by our exuberance.

Flying along, flat out at forty-five mph, (on the flat that is) I soon discovered that if we were going to pass anything it would be very difficult, as it would mean my easing out into the passing lane and relying on my co-driver to give me the okay to pass. Imagine for a minute, if you will, the fact that I would be fully in the passing lane before I would see oncoming traffic.

Fortunately for me, Jenny was only able to pass cyclists, so we were overtaken, even by little old ladies, who only drove to church on Sundays. (slight exaggeration) We were having fun however, that was the main thing, had it been a Rolls Royce, I am certain the joy would not have been much less.

Two and a half hours later we arrived in Smith Falls, drove into a park by the water, spread out a blanket, opened the brown bags of sandwiches and poured the tea, and then enjoyed a meal fit for a king.

To journey further would not be for this day, so we decided to rest on our laurels for now, and enjoy what we had.

My love informed me and she would really like an ice cream, and although we could write at that moment forward to, data in the week one of those cones might be of more importance, that easy inference above, sharing a cone, it just came natural to us.

We returned to Kingston, which must have been a little more downhill on the way back, as we shaved a full five minutes of the time. Our landlady sat on the steps as we drew up, Iris looked a little embarrassed realizing she had to say we only got as far as Smiths Falls.

"You are so soon back," said the landlady

"We only got to Smith falls" Iris replied

Her reply came as no surprise:

"I am not surprised in that thing!" Pointing to our proud possession she went on to say "did you have a good time though, you both deserved it."

"We had a wonderful day together, we really did." Iris said in all sincerity.

CHAPTER 15

New Horizons

With the course nearing the end, the instructors were continually prompting us that we needed a typing skill of thirty words per minute this with under one and a half percent errors, and of course an average of eighty-five to pass the course, so we were all kept on our toes. My typing was better than that, that is, until the instructor brought out his stopwatch, unfortunately that was enough to lower my speed, and increase my error margin.

Another interesting factor was that we were awaiting our postings across Canada, and these were expected any day. My wife and I, had discussed this with reference to Jenny, and the thought of having to drive any great distance at all with her, was scary, to say the least.

We continued using the weekends to take limited trips, so we were using our wheels to good use. Taking a trip to Syracuse, we were told, in New York State, with $200, would really set you up.

My love thought this would be an excellent chance to go there before our posting, wherever that might be. We would need an overnight pass, as it needed a 200-mile return journey. Gas was not really a factor, as her one redeeming feature was that Jenny would run forever, it seemed, on a tank of gas.

Leaving off work on the Friday night, we made our way over the Thousand Island Bridge to Watertown in N.Y. State, and proceeded down Interstate 85, prepared to drive as long as it took to reach our destination.

Fellow travellers got quite a lift as they passed us, honking, waving and laughing, some of them even giving us rude gestures. It must have been scary for them at times, to see the lady, on the normal side as the driver, busily combing her hair, or applying lipstick, with both hands on her face or head. The gestures were easy to answer, as, if I gave the gas pedal a sharp push, the exhaust would give out a suitable rude reply, this developed into quite a game.

As this was our first trip to the USA, we approached customs on our return to Canada with a little trepidation, we had a little stuff in plastic bags, and had filled out the necessary forms, but Iris felt uncomfortable. Not that she was worried about that side of it, as we were still well within our limit. However, a strip search would have been, to say the least, embarrassing, as how would she explain the two dresses with a sweater on top, feeling cold, I think not.

Our fears were groundless, as he waved us through, after making reference to our cars name, and enjoying a laugh.

Final examinations began, and according to our instructors we would not be informed of our future destinations until we had passed. We awaited the results of each separate test with bated breath, and it was a definite relief to finally know that I had passed.

We had to wait one more day for our postings to be announced. Our names were called out, followed by our destination, I heard some fascinating places being announced, at last it came:

"Swash, Fredericton N.B."

I did not realize at that moment, but my life was about to change drastically.

I hurried home to inform Iris, who was patiently waiting to find out just where we would be putting our hat next. I must admit, there were more exotic places we had dreamed of, at least we were not going back to Nova Scotia, for, after all, you do join the Army to see the world, is that not right.? Scrutinizing a map later we realized that N.B. was far too much of a task for our Jenny.

It had been agreed upon by Ottawa, that, as I to had paid for my wife to come to Kingston, they would not pay for our next move.

We had a lot of trouble trading poor old Jenny in, but we left our Fartin Jenny in her adopted home, in exchange for another English vehicle, a Morris Oxford. In the short time we had used her, she had made many happy memories of our expeditions, which, as you can read, are still with us.

CHAPTER 16

Maine New Hampshire and Freedom

My final day in Vimy barracks consisted of me reading and signing my course report, which would precede me to my new destination. I mention this as, while signing, I reread the last few remarks on my basic training report:

"This man does not have the necessary requirements to be considered for promotion." It said.

"How wrong," I thought, that jumped up little 2Lt would be.

It was a brisk sunny autumn morning as we crossed from Cornwall, Ontario into N.Y. State. We had planned to traverse the route through the USA, rather than Québec as we had already seen that Province from the train. We took highway number 2, which eventually brought us to Bangor in Maine, where we would be re-entering N.B.

This small country road, by American standards, was interspersed with small towns and villages, which made for a quaint and interesting trip. Progressing into Vermont, New Hampshire and Maine, the beauty of the changing leaves was a joy to see. We took the utmost from every minute of each others company, to enjoy this incredible treat, it was the holiday we had never had, it seemed.

Fredericton, the provincial capital of New Brunswick, actually is a very nice place. However, to us, arriving on a cold wet day, which coincidently was their half day closing, yes! they used to do that. We formed a less than idyllic impression of the city than we otherwise would have done.

This opinion was further exemplified by the difficulty we were having, to find accommodation. We literally had to go door to door, before a widow lady with no previous thought of renting, took pity on us, and we were once again in a one room, apartment with kitchen privileges.

My new employment was in the teletype facility, where we processed messages from the East for onward transmission to Ontario and the West. The work was interesting, and more importantly, my reaction to my superiors and peers were good. My Iris had obtained employment with the Dominion store, and she was also happy in her environment.

The good part of travelling around is, that there are always new fields to conquer, so when ever we were free, we were out seeing the countryside. Christmas was approaching. This was an aphrodisiac to my wife, and it really was a season of joy and happiness.

We had no plans to share the holiday time with anyone, but that never dampened our feelings, as we never seemed to get fed up with being in each other's company. So, the thought of going to my unit's Christmas party, followed by the store party on another evening, was high on our agenda.

My party day arrived, and it was freezing cold, I had been working the day shift, and change over time was at 4 PM. One of my fellow workers had invited me to drop in to meet his wife, and have a drink. As I had a 90-minute wait for Iris to finish, I thought this was an excellent idea, as maybe he and his wife could join us later on in the evening.

The outside of the store was very slippery, and as my love came through the door in a great hurry, I watched, as her feet slipped from under her, and she crashed down on her back. I rushed to help her up, but her pride was hurt more than her body, or that is what she was trying to portray.

As I bent down to assist her to her feet, she smelled my breath, and her humiliation got the better of her:

"I have been slaving my guts out, while you were out drinking."

she was livid. (I knew this instantly, by her use of the word guts, as I knew that word was not in her vocabulary.)

Trying to explain that I had only had one drink, did nothing to appease her anger. We had, of course, had minor skirmishes before, but this was a serious confrontation, as her pride had been hurt, consequently we never did arrive at the party.

By the time her party came along, and the tiff was long forgotten. I know she was sorry for me, that we had not attended my little affair, as she knew in the Army, although it was a party, it is taken as a parade which one must attend.

We did not know at this time, that fate was already playing its part in our future. Camp Sussex, about 80 miles south east of Fredericton, was the training camp for the Black Watch Regiment of Canada.

The corporal in charge of the signal detachment at the camp, was in serious trouble with the regiment. They wanted him out of there, and they wanted him out "Now," as his influence on the recruits was not in accordance with their requirements. The Camp Commander demanded from my Commanding Officer that they send a junior

Cpl., one who would recognize his responsibilities in a training facility.

I was completely ignorant of this problem, until being called into the office, of the CO and told that I would be off to Camp Sussex the next morning, to assume the duties of the detachment corporal. This came as a complete surprise to me, as I was the junior signalman in the office.

Apparently, the CO had asked all of the shift supervisors who they would recommend, and it was almost unanimous in my favour. The problem was, it was a restricted posting, which meant that I could not take my wife with me. This took part of the shine off the ginger bread, my days in Fredericton were over.

CHAPTER 17

Peace and Tranquility

My joy and excitement over my promotion, along with the increase in our financial standing, were negated only by the fact that we would be parted for a while. A promise, if a promise had even been needed, was the fact that I would find a home somewhere, somehow, and quickly end our separation.

I reported in at my new destination, had a tour of the signal's complex with my predecessor – this took all of 10 minutes, as I had not exactly taken over the largest communication facility in the Canadian Army – nonetheless, I was the boss!

He introduced me to the telephone lineman, who was responsible for the telephone system in the camp, and to one of my four female telephone operator who was on duty that day. One of the missing operators, I was quick to learn, would soon attempt to, how do they say it:

"Wrap me around her finger."

As soon as I had settled in, I returned to the camp orderly room, the heart of the operations, and asked a clerk if she knew of any accommodation in the Sussex area.

"I will make some inquiries," she said, "It is not easy."

That afternoon, I met the Regimental Sergeant Major "Whispering Smith," as he was affectionately called, not to his face however. He marched me in to be introduced to my new Major, who promptly informed me:

"You had better be more cooperative than that Cpl. you are replacing, or you will be soon be back to join him in Fredericton."

To be forewarned is to be forearmed, I had no intention of being other than an ideal NCO. The following morning, the lady in the orderly room, greeted me with some kind words:

"I heard of a place last night," she said, "it might not be suitable for you, but here is the telephone number and the address."

I immediately rang for an appointment, and during my lunch break, I tore off into Sussex to meet a dear old couple in their eighties, as their name Magee, she definitely had to be Irish. She showed me this little place adjoining her property.

In their young days, it had been a small store, now it had been converted into a one-bedroom apartment, with a small sitting room and kitchen. It was built right on top of the ground, the bedroom was very small, the living room was adequate and sparsely furnished, the kitchen had one huge iron oven, which was fueled by wood, for general cooking and baking purposes.

The living room was heated by an oil drip heater, which turned out to be a constant nightmare, not exactly pioneer living, but close. This resulted a few weeks later, with a visit from the fire brigade, nothing serious.

It was clean, not the Ritz, however, I felt that with Iris's touch it would soon be livable, and as beggars cannot be choosers, I happily signed on. Then as I proceeded back to camp I wondered for a moment,

"Would my Iris like it?"

Now I had to get the wheels of bureaucracy moving, and get the move okayed from Ottawa. Surprisingly and thankfully, the powers that be, made the application right away, and it was almost the first message I sent from my new command.

I immediately informed her of what I had done, so she gave in her notice of leaving at the store, on the next day she was surprised when the store manager told her:

"If you are interested, there is a position for you in the Sussex store, he then went on to say, "You can leave whenever you like."

That weekend the Morris Oxford was up to Fredericton and back in very short order, united we stand, divided we fall, could very well be our motto. Once again, I had her with me.

Long before the application for authority came through, one of my first incoming messages was to inform me that I had been promoted three weeks before I was actually eligible, not to worry:

"Keep the stripes on your arm, and do three weeks unpaid," they said.

If only I could meet that 2Lt now! Never get promoted eh!

What I am going to divulge this instance, seems, I know, as a departure from the truth, it is however, an honest fact, just one more coincidence that followed me through my life.

I received instructions that I was to report to Fredericton for a staff meeting the following week. Proceeding down the hallway past the CO's office, he called out,

"Cpl Swash, I would like you to meet Capt. (?),"

I cannot remember his name. Apparently, he had just been promoted, and posted here as the junior communications officer,

"Captain, I would like you to meet my newest corporal."

You have probably guessed by now, it was:

"Old Sour Guts," my recent basic training officer.

He grunted unhappily:

"Pleased to meet you Cpl." Of course, he was. Ha.!

What ever you may think, that was not a figure of my imagination.

CHAPTER 18

Kilts Drums and Agony Bags

This was an extremely pleasant time for us, Sussex, the Dairy Capital of Sussex, was beautiful, the valleys and dales were a picture of tranquility. I was soon involved with the camp activities, as, at my first mess meeting, I was duly elected, without dissent, the president of the J.N.C.O.'s club.

I was elected, "railroaded" was a truer definition, no one wanted the job, and the decision was made long before we opened the meeting.

Of course, this made my better half the "first lady," a good excuse for an extra new dress now and then. She never ever let me down, there was never a time when I wasn't proud to show her off.

Have you ever wondered what Scotsmen wear under there kilts.? As the President, if, I was not aware of it before, I was soon to find out. The Black Watch have two sporrans, the first of which is their dress sporran, worn only on special occasions. Composed of an overlay of white hair, with added silver adornments, it is very Imposing.

The daily, or work sporran, is simply a brown leather bag worn, as I am sure you are all aware of, is in the front of the kilt, below the waist. This combined with a drink or two, becomes a problem, as the dress code allows them to remove this addition when engaged in social activities.

When we held our dances, or such functions, my main job as the president was to continually warn inebriated members to sit in a suitable manner. Ladies are born to observe this decorum, men, on the other hand, forget when they are inappropriately covered. The "crown jewels" is not exactly a pretty sight, so now you know there are no garments beneath a true Scots kilt.

All regiments except the Scottish, use bugles to sound the various calls necessary to run a military camp, "Reveille" and "Lights out," for instance, instead the Black Watch, use Bagpipes (agony bags, if you are not from the land of the Thistle.) while they may sound very stirring, or even plaintiff, when playing "Amazing Grace" I can assure you that played repeatedly right under your window, a dozen times a day can be most disturbing.

At this time, fate would play another factor in our life, as, on one Saturday night during a social evening, an honorary member, with whom a we had made friends, suggested we go down to Martin's Head on the Bay of Fundy, following the end of the dance.

He informed us that they often did this, they built a fire when they got there, toasted marshmallows for the kids, roughed it in the car for what was left of the night, and in the morning fished for Flounders. It sounded different, so we went along, going home first to collect some food, as they had suggested, and met them later.

He led the way, down a dirt track, with room for only one vehicle at a time, for forty or so miles. Finally, we arrived at the beach, and did the things mentioned earlier. He had checked the tides, and they were appropriately low just after six. If you have not been to the Bay of Fundy, it is known through out the world for its "tidal bore."

The tide comes in so fast; it creates a head of water which precedes it right up to Moncton, and beyond, truly it is of vacationer's must-see event. At low tide the mud, for that is what it is, stretches for a great distance, as the Bay all but empties, and it leaves behind huge mounds and valleys of mud, similar to the sand dunes in the desert.

We were at the mercy of our friend, who had furnished us with fishing poles. The party of two men, two women, and three children, one in her mother's arms, set out clambering up and over these muddy obstructions, until we reached the water.

Putting our lines out, we were very soon engrossed, pulling in these flatfish, oblivious to our surroundings. My better half, who, I had mentioned earlier was always conscious of the sea, suddenly she cried out:

"Look, we are almost cut off."

The tide was swirling through the valleys of mud, so we quickly ditched the tackle and fish, and rushed to get back to the beach. Each division between the mounds had gotten deeper and faster with rushing water, as we neared the shore, it was purely a matter of time

We men took turns carrying the baby while spurring the others on, eventually, by God's good grace, we made the beach. A few minutes longer, and we would have been swept helplessly with the tide. The God's had been good to us.

My wife and I were so subdued on our return journey, she held my hand in the car, and I knew she, like me, realized we had just survived a turn in our lives.

CHAPTER 19

A Fly in the Ointment

Life proves to us at every turn that nothing is ever perfect, Camp Sussex, was no exception to this rule. In the previous chapter I made mention of a telephone operator, "wrap me around your finger, Flo," was her name.

This lady had served in the Signal Corps in World War II where she had met and married an Officer, but was soon on her way to a divorce. She had managed to get herself involved with several of her serving comrades, one of whom she claimed, was my commanding officer in Fredericton.

Her mode of operation here in Sussex, was to avail herself to her immediate superior, thus putting his feet to the fire when she pulled one of her favourite tricks.

It was not long before I received invitations to visit her apartment to have a drink, and no doubt, engage in a clandestine relationship. This was not a part of my makeup, so my refusals began to develop into a confrontational atmosphere.

She was not, in fact, "after my body," it was rather the control it would give her. She was forever taking advantage of the civil service contract. This enabled her to take off single sick days, not to be mistaken for the additional days she was allowed without a doctor's certificate.

Please "call in's "always came in at the most in inopportune moments, leaving me to scramble around for a replacement. I had, in fact, been forced to learn the operation of the switchboard to enable me to fill in, in an emergency.

The climax came one evening, an hour before she was to report for the Midnight shift. I already had one operator on leave, which meant that the operator on duty would have to work overtime.

This meant the operator on duty would be required to perform her duties for 16 hours in a 24-hour period. I took the watch, adamant in my own mind, that this problem would be resolved.

The following day, "Flo" shows up for her watch.

"Oh," she says, "What a time I had yesterday!"

The master of deception was playing her role to the full.

"I was in this mall, and I collapsed suddenly, they called for an ambulance, and I was taken to the hospital, where I spent the night."

"Not a bad excuse, eh? One big problem, I did not believe her.

"Glad you are better now," I said, "are you okay to work?"

She assured me she was and, confident that she had once again pulled the wool over someone's eyes, she took her place in the office.

We had a Signals detachment in St. Johns New Brunswick, where this supposed event had transpired. I signalled the boss there to find out for me if an incident such as this had indeed taken place in the mall, and for him to contact the hospital to see if a patient had been admitted.

It was not long before I had my answer in writing on my teletype machine.

"No" to the first and "No" to the second, in addition he had contacted the other hospital in St. John, in case her fuddled brain had caused her another amnesia attack, he again replied to the negative.

When confronted, Florence flew into a rage screaming:

"I can't go for an (expletive) without you knowing!"

The resulting disciplinary action was long forthcoming, and extremely light when it did arrive.

My life in the office was never disturbed again by Flo! and subsequently her attention record was impeccable. When I got home, Iris thought this episode was hilarious, she never conceived a person could go to such lengths to concoct an excuse of that magnitude.

CHAPTER 20

A Visitor

Once again normalcy had returned to the office, and we were able to enjoy the comforts of our existence. The Magee's, who I mentioned earlier, had become like a father and mother to us. My better half, who was an excellent cook in her own right, was having some difficulty with the old wood burning monster in the kitchen.

No modern knobs to turn on, enabling you to adjust the heat on this old wood veteran. Anything prepared on the top was no trouble, you just moved the appliance to a cooler spot, baking however, was much more difficult, this is where our landlady came in, she led Iris through the intricacies of this veteran of the cooking wars.

In no time, I was coming home to the smell of fresh baked bread, rolls, apple pies, and cookies, all tempting to my palate.

The oil drip heater was not as satisfying, as it was made up of large metal pipes about a foot in diameter which circulated in a maze, just below the ceiling, as they led from the living room, and into the bedroom.

One evening as we were sitting talking and reading, we had no television set at that time. When we noticed a burning kind of smell, on investigating we discovered that the pipe leading into the bedroom was red hot and glowing for about 3 feet.

We had the fire service there in short time, and they had quite a problem lowering the heat in the pipe.

From then on, we were much more apprehensive of the heating system than we were previously. If you know New Brunswick at all, in the winter time, you must have heat.

Around that time my wife drew my attention to an advertisement in the local paper for a contest with a bakery in Moncton. They required you to say in 25 words or less why their bread was the best. The first prize was a weekend in New York city, the second was a television set, which we could surely use,

"Use your talents," Iris chided, with this in mind, I spent some time dreaming up an idea. It went something like this,

Appetizing smell, Appealing sight, Light touch, Quality hearing and Delicious taste

Making for a sixth sense:

"Make Lane's bread your bread."

Iris put her John Henry on it, and several weeks later she made her TV debut, appearing on a Moncton television station, accepting a Sylvania television set.

The latest technology of the day.

The first prize would have been a waste of time, and over in three days, so who says your prayers are not answered.?

As I sat in an adjoining room watching the program on a monitor, the thought that I had written the entry, and that she was in there taking the glory, never even occurred to me.

She looked as lovely, as ever, and carried herself with grace and dignity. I was proud just viewing her performance, which, this in itself, was sufficient fame for me.

This event had hardly come to place when I received the information that I was to attend a Junior N.C.O course for six weeks, I knew it was coming, as part of the terms for my promotion was that I must pass this course to keep my stripes.

Fortune shined us again with this one, as the course could have been anywhere in Canada, it turned out to be on my very own doorstep. This did not mean I had an advantage, as the instructors would come from some other military establishment, but I would be close to home.

The course took six weeks, and It was similar to taking basic training all over again, with the exception we had to be able to perform as, drill instructors, give classroom lessons to the fellow students, and learn about military law etc.

This time I found it challenging, and I entered it with enthusiasm, after all, I had no intention of losing my promotion. We were not allowed off camp, however, Iris was not banned from coming to the corporal's mess, so we met whenever possible. Of course, there were no intimate contacts as we had been getting Saltpeter in our tea and coffee, there were no problems in that direction.

We had been toying with the idea of getting Iris's mother over from England for a visit, as her father had recently passed away. This meant we needed different accommodation, as this place was too small.

Mrs. Magee had shed a lot of tears when we announced this decision to her. As we had made quite an impression on her, and she on us, it was very difficult for us to come up with this resolution.

CHAPTER 21

Storm Clouds Arising

We had decided to postpone the visit of Iris's mother for a while, she was not too sure about coming over, and there were looming complications on this side of the ocean

In the Middle East, the future was evolving rapidly, with Sadat and his forces taking on the Israelis. He quickly realized it was a huge mistake on his part, when the Jewish state accepted his challenge.

Meanwhile in England and France were being troubled over the security of the Suez Canal, they dispatched a large military force to the area. This made for a tension filled atmosphere within the forces of all nations.

Prime Minister Lester Pearson ruled that, as soon as the United Nations Expeditionary Forces were formed, Canada, and, particularly the Royal Canadian Signal Corps, would make up a large proportion of the participating countries.

This event took place in 1956, and I found myself on the initial draft to set up the communications network for the other nations. The draft was slated to go to Halifax and sail on H.M.C.S. Bonaventure.

I was prepared to be away for at least a year, a year from my home. I can say truthfully, that the prospect did not thrill me one bit, as

Egypt was a place from my previous service during the war, which had left me with no desire to ever return.

A reprieve of some sort came for me in the form, that, any member of the Canadian contingent who spoke with a British accent, was to be removed from the draft, for precautionary measures, it being felt the recent British occupation of the canal could place us in jeopardy.

"Joy to the world," maybe I had dodged this bullet, only time would prove otherwise. It soon became obvious that the duration of the UN force would be one year, and it was equally plain that I would figure in the draft in 1957.

We ensured that we made the most of our time together, leading to a trip to the United States of America, which would have made less immortals cringe.

We had decided that, to make the trip, which included visiting Boston, it would be advantageous to get a larger car, as it was a long trip and required reliable transportation. We looked around and saw a 1953 Chevrolet, it looked to be in really good condition, and was only three years old.

Our friend of the Fundy days had a business in Sussex, and he alternately purchased a car one year, and a truck the next from this same dealer. He suggested that it might be in our interest to take him along for bargaining power.

The dealer turned us away from the one we wanted, recommending a 1951 Chevrolet, at the same time advising us that this one was a much better buy, and cheaper. He claimed it had been completely overhauled, and he added that the engine was in tiptop condition, and would not let us down.

"You had better be right, or I do not come back next year" my friend said.

"Would I lie to you?" he said.

We have never trusted a car dealer since.

Our first day saw us half way between St. John, New Brunswick and the border in Maine, a desolate stretch of highway, or it was in those days. "Pst Pst" the gauge said half a tank of gas remained, not being mechanically minded, I had no idea what was troubling our new bought bomb!

A friendly motorist stopped to offer us assistance, from my description of the events leading up to this stop, led him to believe it was out of gas, despite the gauge reading.

He got under the car and said:

"Your problem is that your tank has been hit by a large rock, right where the gauge is, your car will always register half a tank when your empty."

He took me to the nearest gas station to get some gas, brought me back, and stayed around until the engine was running. Not too often that this happens now, the good Samaritan act I mean, this is New Brunswick and the natives were like that.

We got through the customs at Calais, Maine, and proceeded down the coast road, the temporary hiccup behind us. We drove into Portland, which is quite a large city. I cruised up to a red light at a busy intersection, which was on quite a rise, and stopped.

The gear shift was stuck, this left me no option but to ask the following driver if he would kindly give me a push through the intersection. At first, he was reluctant to do this, as he had a new automobile, however, he had little choice if he wanted to proceed on his way. Returning to the car, and placing my foot down on the clutch, we resumed our ill-fated journey.

The level ground seemed to suit this gearshift, so we proceeded on our merry way. Cruising down the next steep hill, the gearshift jumped out of gear, and repeated this function, each and every time we had a chance to coast. To say my better half was mad, would be putting it mildly,

"It wouldn't have happened if we had bought that other Chevy." She said, almost in tears.

"Why did we take John (the friend) with us?"

Her reference to the salesman does not bear repeating. I felt awful, I wanted the trip to be so wonderful in case we were in for a year or more separation.

We had planned our second stop to be at Kennebunkport on the coast, I expect it was my military background, but planning was a part of my vacation that I enjoyed. Approximately 50 miles short of this point, the car started to make a horrible noise, I knew enough to know it was the muffler causing this din.

Pulling over onto the soft shoulder I got out and took a cursory look, the pipe was having a love affair with the tarmac, this was enough to turn the air blue, I was so mad and disappointed.

I knew right then that Boston was out of the question. I got a piece of wire from a house nearby and temporarily fixed it up, and proceeded to our first stop, where I would get it repaired.

CHAPTER 22

Blue Skies and Warm Winds

We were just about due for a break in our fortunes, the day had been filled with downturns and problems, could it get any worse.? As we reached our destination, the sun was setting, we were tired, and anxious to find a place to rest and relax.

We were fortunate enough to find a small unit in a motel complex, with a kitchenette, superior to some of the bedsitter's we had called home. The cost was only seven dollars a night, six, if you stayed longer. We took it for one night only, as our dream vacation was still to be Boston. However, we still had to visit the garage the next morning, so our continuance from here, was still up in the air.

Rising early, we strolled down to the beach, which was very conveniently close, only one block away. The sun was shining from a clear blue sky, we linked arms, as we strolled along the water's edge, the world and Egypt, seemed miles away, this was the life! Why could it not always be like this.?

On returning to our motel, we prepared to go out to pick up our disappointing vehicle, from its visit to the mechanic, Iris said,

"You had better check the oil,"

"Why" I asked, "It has just had an engine overall."

"I would rather you did," she went on,

We discovered in a hurry, that the rest of what the salesman had told us was a lot of lies.

I raised the hood, removed and cleaned the dipstick, replaced it, and took it out again to check, she was right again, just the merest signs of oil could be seen, we had bought the Lemon of the century.! The mechanic could only repair the muffler, so, after hearing our story, he advised us to drive very carefully back home, and then confront this salesman with all the details.

The bill was not large by today's standards, but it had made a deep hole in our vacation money, this was money that we had not taken into consideration.

I was determined that I was not going to let this spoil our holiday. Boston was out, but what was wrong with this paradise. We booked for the next six days, left the car - for want of a better name - in the parking lot, and availed ourselves of the many beautiful facilities Kennebunkport had to offer.

This holiday has remained in my memory more vividly, than many we have had since, there were times when we were more financially sound. money does not buy happiness, love for each other does. The return journey was less stressful, our confrontation with the dealer resulted in our actually getting a new engine replaced,

"All's well that ends well," not quite!

Six months had passed, so we arranged for my Mother-in-law to come over for a year, this meant, if I had to go to Egypt, she would have six months alone with her daughter, and they could go back to England together until my tour of duty was over. At the time we made this arrangement, neither of us realized how important these dates would be.

The dreaded message arrived, my posting to UNEF Egypt was

firm. I was to leave Montréal, Dorval Airport for a one-year tour to the Middle East.

Although we both had expected it, the news was not received with any kind of jubilation. To add further insult to injury, I had a fear of flying, and here I was faced with an added disappointment, no nice sea trip on the Bonaventure.

I was fully convinced in my own mind that this was it, I would not return. To say that I was apprehensive would be putting it mildly.

Iris drove me up to Fredericton, where I boarded the train for the barracks in Montréal. It was more than a normal goodbye, see you in a year, for me. I hugged and kissed her as if it were for the last time. She often told me in later years, that she could feel on that day that I really thought it was our final farewell. I hung out of the train window until she disappeared from view.

CHAPTER 23

Unwanted Babysitter

The train gathered speed, rapidly distancing me from my love, rushing me ever forward to an unwanted and uncertain future. I found myself gazing out of the window, not noticing anything, my mind completely taken up with my life so far.

Would I ever see her face again? hold her in my arms? had I told her enough times what I thought I wondered? I caught a glimpse of my face in the window, and I thought to myself, as I had said many times before,

"What did she ever see in me?"

Unfortunately, the thought of her being unfaithful while I was away, had not left me.

The journey was uneventful, and I found myself at last in Montréal. I flagged down a taxi, as I remembered from my past experience that you had to find your own way in the Canadian Army!

"Longeueil Camp driver," I ordered

After being directed to my room in the barracks, I found, that apart from one other service man, a member of the Royal Canadian Engineers, we were the only two inhabitants left in the premises.

He quickly unloaded on me how happy his marriage was, how

much he loved his two children, and that he was not a carouser, and not fond of beer, he did seem a suitable fellow traveller.

When he suggested that we go down to see the sights in the city, as neither of us had been previously in Montréal, I agreed. Why did I acquiesce.? He had, however, forgot to tell me he was also a liar!

We had only just arrived on Catherine's Street, when he suggested going into a bar for a beer, I readily agreed, as I was not against an occasional ale to be sociable. Finishing that drink in much quicker time than I would normally would have done, we continued our sightseeing.

It was not long before we came upon a glittering edifice offering, "Strippers, Strippers come on in."

My associate's eyes lit up like a Christmas tree, he gave off the impression he had never seen a woman in a provocative position before. He was inside the joint before I could even blink an eye:

"Two beers," he said without even asking me.

You could hardly see the stage for cigarette smoke, the place was full of ogling men, calling out comments to the participating girls, after a while I finally made out the images, I must admit, they did have shapely bodies, and were adequately supplied in all the right places.

This place, I thought, would settle my companion down for a while, so I suggested to him that we get a cab back to the depot. He was obviously enjoying the sights and sounds, so we had another beer.

After an hour of this display, it began to get monotonous, the girls changed, but the show continued in the same format, maybe getting just a little raunchier.

The engineer had obviously had enough to drink, and I found out he had been reinforcing his intake without my knowledge.

"I am getting a taxi, with or without you." I said,

Actually, I had no intention of leaving him to his own devices, not in this locality. Eventually I got him out onto the street, but before I could get a grip on him, he had shot upstairs to another Bistro.

I was livid with myself, that I had got into such a predicament, but I could not leave him, as he was dangerous to himself. I did not know the half of it.

Upon reaching the top of the stairs the drunken bum was having an argument with some real tough looking customers. I got between him and them, forcing him down the stairs behind me, it was then that the roughnecks started to follow us.

My Marine training came out after a while, and before I realized it, I had undone my military belt, with the large brass buckle.

I faced them, prepared to use it if necessary. The best thing of the night happened when we reached the sidewalk, the antagonists had not decided to give up, and were still in hot pursuit. However there, on the sidewalk, stood one of "Montréal's finest." I handed my stupid comrade to him for safe custody, while I hailed a taxi

On our return to camp, I checked the noticeboard for the following days departures, he was listed to fly the next day, I was not, I wasn't sorry about that.

The airlift was scheduled in such a way, that every two days an RCAF Yukon transport plane left Dorval for the Azores. On arriving, it unloaded the passengers from Montréal, it then took on the troops from the previous flight, leaving those that had just arrived, to spend two days in a Portuguese military camp.

The flight then continued on, to land at Gibraltar, before journeying on to an Air Force base close to Naples, Italy.

My flight, was two days after my fiasco in Montréal, and I made sure I did not put myself in a similar position again. The bus took us to Dorval, where I got my first real close up look of the aircraft. It did not look any safer to me, regardless of the distance I was from it.

I gazed at it with absolute trepidation, it was not the first time in my life that I had faced danger, but this was of a different kind, "Physiological," an inner fear, an anxiety over which I had no control.

As everything in the military is done in the same manner, an officer commenced to call out our names and seat numbers, so, with that, we filed on board. My stomach was doing such a twisting and turning, I marvelled that I had not left a brown trail all the way to my seat. A slight exaggeration, of course.

My assigned seat was by a window, but my eyes travelled everywhere, but looking out of it. We began to taxi to the takeoff position. My thoughts were back in Sussex, I realized I had my fists clenched, I heard the roar of the engines, felt myself forced ever so slightly back into the seat, we had reached, in my mind "the point of no return."

It took me fully half an hour to peek out of a window, gradually looking down a bit at a time, until finally I saw the land beneath me. So far so good.

I would like to say right now, that I have travelled many miles by air since then, but the fear is not much better.

Chapter 24

Count to Ten

Eventually arriving in the Azores and taking in the sights for two days, my next boarding day arrived. An hour into the flight, the pilot came on the intercom to inform us that the weather in Gibraltar, was not good enough for landing, so were being diverted to a French naval base in French Morocco.

We landed on the base at lunch hour, where the Chef was proud to announce that we had come on the right day, as they were serving Escargot and frog legs. These were the first, for most of us, and surprisingly an enjoyable delicacy, my thoughts were not shared by all however.

Our location was below the desert area of Morocco, and was tropical forest, it was really green and lush. The humidity was very high, and it was most uncomfortable.

On landing, our pilot told us we would not be able to take off until four pm as we would get heavy rainfall in the afternoon. This is a daily occurrence, and something to behold.

On time, the pilot had us airborne again, heading north to resume our next stage of flight. I would like to say, that I was now, more at ease, I had opened my clenched fist, so there was some improvement, however, any regaining of my confidence was short-lived.

The Yukon, without completely shutting down its engines, discharged its human cargo, taxied off, and headed back to Gibraltar.

We all gathered on the tarmac, wondering what had happened, only to be informed that the airport in El Arish in the Gaza Strip was temporarily shut down.

They then told us that we would be going by alternate means, and to report back the following morning at eight am. Buses then took us to an Italian camp for the night I should have known I was in trouble, when we were met the next morning, to give us a 30-minute parachute course?"

He had to be kidding I thought, but he wasn't. He instructed us how to bend our knees on impact, how to roll when we hit the ground, and the scariest part was when he said:

"When you come down in water it is hard to judge the distance, so do not pull the ripcord too early."

With this part completed, we were issued with parachutes, if my thoughts of never returning home needed any further enhancing, this had to be it. Just for a minute my mind went back home, what would her feelings be if she knew what was happening over here?

The next thing to appear was a 119 Twin Fuselage airplane, known as a "Box Car." This plane was used by the airborne for ferrying Paratroopers to their drop targets. The Sgt was obviously having a great time at our expense, as he went on to tell us:

"If it got into trouble, the plane would not glide like a normal aircraft, it would go into a spiral and crash" he went on to say:

"That is why we in the airborne use it,"

That is why passengers are required to carry parachutes in the ready position at all times," he continued.

We eventually took off for El Arish in this rattletrap of a plane, we were seated in uncomfortable bucket seats along each side, hooked up to a line for the parachute. The Sgt was then asked:

"What if I don't want to jump," someone asked

"When the first guy goes, you all go, think yourselves lucky, I am the last." He was really enjoying this.

During this exercise, he unhooked us one by one and took us to the jumping platform in the rear, this was an iron trap door, with, I swear, only an inch or more gap in the middle. He told us to look down through it.

My stomach came up into my mouth, it looked big enough to fall through, of course it wasn't. I was not the only passenger who quickly disembarked, when we eventually landed in Egypt. If there had been no one around, I would have knelt down and kissed the ground like the Pope, I was that relieved.

CHAPTER 25

Egypt

Nothing had changed in the 14 years that had passed since I was last in this country. Immediately upon setting foot on the tarmac, we were besieged by kids pedaling, shoe shines, camel hide wallets, and other assortments of trinkets.

They looked like identical twins to me, of the kids who had pestered me everywhere on my previous tour. "Imshi Igri" I yelled, at one particularly obnoxious beggar,

"You English Basted," he yelled back at me,

He shot me a look of hatred, when, here I was, speaking in his native tongue, and I still could not hide my British heritage.

Is it no wonder all the Canadian forces speaking with a British accent were deleted from the previous tour of duty? This derogatory term (in English) if it was used and the same circumstances, would draw the same sort of response, sufficient to say, I was left alone from then on.

As the United Nation forces are no longer in existence, I am permitted to lay out in some small detail, how it was set up. The various contingents were located in the Gaza Strip where the long-distance air transport aircraft, and the smaller planes, that were used for local duties, and a communication center.

Forty some odd miles east were the main military headquarters in Rafah, further, east at Gaza city, which housed the headquarters of the UN diplomats. Additional sub-communication centres were scattered all over the Sinai desert.

We were whisked away to Rafah, to be dispersed to where our expertise was needed. My first destination turned out to be in Gaza city, which had the best accommodation. If there was any sweet outcome from being over there, at least I had drawn the best facility to start. Assigned to the office of the CO, I discarded my teletype mantel for the time being, to become his personal clerk.

During my stay here, I made some very useful contacts in the bazaars downtown, which served as well. With these, added to my limited resource of the language, I received a commission from the owners of the stores for directing high spending Canadians to their stores.

One of those, was the mayor of Gaza, who invited me to his home for a meal. I did not meet any of his wives (Harem) as the feminine members are not allowed to be seen by the infidels, the meal was interesting, Goat meat, complete with their offal, something like Haggis, for the main course.

This was followed with sticky, gooey pastries, dripping with honey which were served for dessert. I showed him pictures of my wife, laughingly telling him, she was not for sale, in case he had any ideas of adding her to his collection.

Another benefit of my association with the merchants was, my ability to purchase at bargain prices, brocade, and other lovely materials, to send home to my wife. Later, returning to Canada, I had two beautiful suits made-to-measure from the best material available, at a very minimal charge. It pays to have contacts.

I soon discovered after arriving in Gaza, that if I could find a Ham radio operator in the Sussex area back home, who, in turn, could contact Rafah. There was a Sgt. here, who gave up his spare time arranging schedules for the troops to speak to their loved ones back home.

He certainly was a good Samaritan, as his time was taken up seven days a week, contacting other Ham operators all over Canada. With the difference in the time zones, this meant he gave up considerable amounts of his time between midnight and four am, reuniting families over the air.

Iris made inquiries back home, luck was with us, and in a few weeks, I was driving down to headquarters for a two am conference call with her twice a week.

She found it embarrassing at first, as the operator had to be present at all times, to switch from send to receive. The privilege of hearing each other's voice, soon overcame any embarrassments, and it certainly made the separation just a little bit better.

My three months in Gaza had been almost enjoyable, and the time had passed reasonably quick, a quarter of my stint was behind me.

Alas, my route for rotation came, and I found myself on my way to El Quisesma, considered by many, the worst detachment of them all. Situated eighty miles out in the desert, it was an oasis, consisting of fifty to one thousand palms trees, the only green vegetation upon the horizon.

CHAPTER 26

Boredom Exemplified

I really have to give you a mental picture of my latest spot on God's creation. This oasis, which probably covers about one hundred thousand square acres, of which we took up about one acre. Our small detachment consisted of a mobile radio truck, converted for radio teletype communications, and it was driven by a generator, which could be heard a mile away.

Adjacent to this, was the kitchen and dining room area, fully fitted with a refrigerator and electric stove, it had no permanent cook, however.!

Our living quarters were quite adequate, with a concrete base and wooden frame, which supported the tent covering, (It never rains in the Southern Sinai.)

We were fortunate to have a screen netting, to keep out the creepy, crawly things, these included the bedbugs.

When you got past this, however, our days were spent with reading or playing cards, (utter boredom,) when we were not manning the outpost. It took only one man at a time to do this, so you can see leisure time was plentiful.

"Can you think of anything more boring, or more contributive to make the days pass at a snail's pace?"

Three months was an eternity, and that is what we had to look forward to for the next four months. To make things worse, the crew must have been "mother's darlings," as they could not even boil water, without burning it.

If it didn't fry, it was history. I discovered after I had taken up residence for a few days, that we had a cold cellar, which had been dug deep in the sand, when the detachment was first set up.

It was full of seven-pound cans of jam, mincemeat, canned fruit and many other assorted things. It appeared, no one had ever known how to utilize this stuff. I initiated another duty roster for a daily cook, which meant, along with the hapless forced volunteer, I had to be supervisor every day.

At first this innovation did not exactly infuse the victims with happiness, but after a while, even their own mothers would be proud of them.

The highlight of the week was the day the plane arrived with our supply's, and most importantly our mail.

Eagerly we waited for the plane to fly over the camp, we immediately jumped into the truck and sped away to the nearby makeshift airstrip. from their girlfriends. I was the only one who was married. My wife was really good, she hardly ever missed a day, when she did not write some words to me, my days were so empty, I never missed writing and rereading her letters.

Once a year El Quesiema runs alive with excitement, as it is the mating season for the donkeys and camels. The Bedouins from miles around, congregate at the oasis, letting their livestock run wild. No organized siring by pedigree males, just a help your self process.

The continuing sounds of braying and snorting from morning till nightfall, and then all-night, makes sleep a little difficult, until you get used to it. When the sounds of animal delights begin to subside, the Arabs fold their tents, the men then climb on board their camels or donkeys, while the women walk patiently beside them, and the animals, across the desert. I witnessed this phenomenon the last day before I left. I am so glad I did.

My tour of duty here was finally over, I was on my way back to Al Arish to take over the detachment there, this was not a Mecca of entertainment either, but it was like Disneyland, compared to where I had just come from.

There was one huge advantage with being there, every so often the large planes would go on a training run after being put through their overall checkups. This was done on a seat available procedure, open to all of the servicemen, not just for those on the in El Arish detachment. Our advantage was, that, if there were empty seats, and we could be spared from duty, we could make the flight at a minute's notice.

We eagerly waited for the plane to fly over the camp, we then jumped into the truck, and sped to the nearby makeshift airstrip. It really was a joy to see the looks of each one of them, but especially the words of love from their girlfriends.

I was the only one who was married, my wife was really good, she hardly ever missed a day, when she did not write some words to me, my days were so empty, I never missed writing to her, and rereading her letters.

Once a year El Quesiema runs alive with excitement, as it is the mating season for the donkeys and camels. The Bedouins from miles around, congregate at the oasis, letting their livestock run wild. No organized siring by pedigree males here, just a help your self process.

The continuing sounds of braying and snorting from morning

till nightfall, and then again all-night, makes sleep a little difficult, until you get used to it. When the sounds of animal delights begin to subside, the Arabs fold their tents, the men then climb on board their camels or donkeys, while the women walk patiently beside them, and the animals, across the desert. I witnessed this phenomenon the last day before I left. I am so glad I did.

My tour of duty here was finally over, I was on my way back to Al Arish to take over the detachment there, this was not a Mecca of entertainment either, but it was like Disneyland, compared to where I had just come from.

There was one huge advantage with being there, every so often the large planes would go on a training run after being put through their overall checkups. This was done on a seat available procedure, open to all of the servicemen, not just for those on the in El Arish detachment. Our advantage was, that, if there were empty seats, and we could be spared from duty, we could make the flight at a minute's notice.

CHAPTER 27

Temptation

My first excursion was to Alexandria the gem in the crown of Egypt, a lovely clean city on the Mediterranean Sea. Gorgeous sandy beaches with lots of entertainment. It has a largely Greek population over the Egyptians, this gave it a whole different dimension.

Fortunately, as it turned out, I had chosen my comrades with a little more care than with the Engineer in Montréal. We spent our days sightseeing, including one of King Farouk's palaces, a magnificent edifice.

When I served in Egypt previously, Farouk had been the king. At that time, he had the traits of a tyrant, he shared women by the dozen, and was living high, at the expense of the rabble. It was claimed that he took 90 Piasters out of every hundred for his personal use. A rich Roué indeed.!

Before we left camp, two of my friends and I, had made a pledge that we would not allow ourselves to be caught up with a visit to a brothel, these are readily available in all of the cities in Egypt.

On our first night, we were dining out at a restaurant in the hotel, when one of my friends said:

"Have you seen those three girls sitting at the bar."

I looked over, and it was obvious that they were making themselves available, it was only a matter of time before they would come over.

After a while, they came and introduced themselves. We told them we were not interested, so they were wasting their time. I have to admit they were beautiful looking girls, with everything where it should be. We made the mistake of saying:

"If you just want to have a drink, sit down"

I was surprised when they took up this offer, but as we had made it, we had to follow through. We indulged in a pleasant conversation, and one drink led to another. The one who had seemingly selected me out of the group said:

"Do you dance?"

I replied in the affirmative, as I do like dancing, and here was an opportunity I wouldn't get back in Camp.

It turned out that she was a beautiful dancer, who took every opportunity, to press her leg, and other accoutrements, very close. The perfume was very heavy, and I have to admit, very desirable.

While I was away, one of the other guys had told them:

"We have no intention of taking you home, or to your room, but, if you want to spend the rest of the evening with us, we will enjoy your company."

So, when I returned to the table the deal had already been made.

We all had an enjoyable evening, lots of dancing, maybe a little more drinking than we should've done, so all in all, we were satisfied with that. We had met together in the toilet (the men that is) and we decided we would give them what they would have got, had they pursued their objective. As it would only cost us 300 piastres, nothing lost.

We met on subsequent evenings, with the same arrangement, and everything was going to plan, however, things began to fall apart on our last night, when I foolishly said I would escort her to her room.

It began innocently enough, I put my arms around her and said good night, with every intention that this was as far as it would go. I found myself hanging on a little longer, and the combination of her perfume and the feel of her body, was getting the best of me.

Soon I was caressing those lovely breasts that had been tantalizing me each evening. I was in a battle between my brain and my loins, one was telling me to keep going, while the other was sending a different message altogether. I opened the door!

From then on, I quickly realized which one was winning. I began to undress her, and, at this time, desire was my only intention. I did not stop on my own volition; I was too carried away for that.

There was a tap on the door, and my friends calling out,

"Albert, let's go."

At that moment I was very annoyed, however, we put our clothes back on, I kissed her, and reluctantly said good-bye. I had not only let my friends down; I had almost betrayed my marriage vows.

We were fortunate enough, to have yet another training flight, this time to Athens in Greece, we had four days of sightseeing, including the Acropolis. Athens was another beautiful city, unfortunately at that time, it was under the Leftist government of Papadouris.

The people were extremely anti USA, and they included us, in with the yanks, so we were met with a lot of hostilities in some places. Visiting these marvellous remains of the past, more than compensated for any discomforts offered by the locals. I returned to El Arish to set up a much more pleasant journey.

No temptations this time!

CHAPTER 28

A Break in the Clouds

It was not the solitude and boredom of El Queseima that bothered me, but rather it was the three months I had lost, of being able to hear the voice from my wife back in New Brunswick. Now I was able to make the 2 am journey to Rafah again, and renew this privilege.

One night she greeted me by saying:

"We are coming back to England, is there any chance you can get over for some leave?" I had previously told her that such a leave was possible, as the flight plan for the Yukon's was now via Langar, an RAF airfield just outside of Nottingham, England, instead of Naples.

Fortunately, at this time, I was half way through my one-year tour of duty, and as there were more personnel arriving in El Arish than departing, the chances for a flight were good:

"Give me the dates," I asked,

I had my application on the desk of my Commanding Officer by 0800 hrs. the next morning."

For the next few weeks I was very easy to live with, my spirits were bullied like never before. The only troubling point was, would I get the leave, on the dates that I had requested. I had made plans in my head for our meeting. Everything would be just right.

Fortune shone on me, or was it that fate factor again. I was beginning to feel excited, my spouse, and her mother would arrive in the docks at Tilbury, in Essex, less than twenty miles from my home town. I would be arriving three days before them, giving me time to give my mother some help in the preparation.

Our shopping expedition pleased me no end, but my mother was not half as pleased as me. She had lost my father at the age of 43 and had never remarried, or even thought about it. With that she had been forced to be very frugal from then on, and was marvellous with what she did. We lived out of town, so we walked in on this day, at her request:

"Buses are for lazy people," my mother informed me, when I suggested using the bus that passed by the door, she angrily turned that down

We started out by going up a steep hill, and it was all I could do to keep up with her. When we reached the beginning of the shopping area, Mom took over the list. It was amusing at first, but it soon became frustrating, as she would say,

"We will get this here, then we will go next door for that. She was still not happy as she went on to say:

"We can go down the road a bit, where we can get that cheaper," and so on.

As I said, I did not want anything to crop up to spoil my coming visit with Iris, so, with tongue-in-cheek I went along with this lesson in frugality. The crowning touch, however, came when we were loaded down with bags, and only potatoes were left on the list, Mom said:

"We will get them at so-and-so's,"

"We could have purchased potatoes in almost every store we had already been in" I said.

"That is at the far end of the town, she informed me:

"Why do we need to go there." I growled.

"They are always Halfpenny cheaper," she replied.

I did not want to hurt her feelings, as I had insisted that I would pay for the groceries.

Even with that, I had been continually lectured throughout the trip, that I was buying too much.

However, this was the straw that broke the camels back:

"No way! We get them here," I said.

From her reaction, I must have snapped my reply to her, as I had always been aware, that at times, she could, shall we say, sulk.!

At that moment, I knew where I got it from, mom was not happy, and I did not further improve her situation by hailing a taxi.

The day of the ship's arrival dawned, and even though I had been told the time of arrival, I was there long before it came down the Thames, as it would not be easy to locate disembarking passengers. The arrival lounge was crowded with people. So, I situated myself an equal distance from the two doors coming out of the Customs outlet, and waited. It was some help to me that they allowed returning British subjects to land first. My wife was able to use this privilege, as we had not yet taken out our citizenship, and she was travelling on her British passport.

I had mentioned that Iris's mother originally came from the same town as I did, so this worked out perfectly. She could stay with her relatives for a few days, then we would take her back to her home, and finish off our dream vacation there. We retired that night, on disrobing, my better half grinned and said:

"I have put on a little weight,"

I had noticed, but this was not the place to start a dialogue on "weight watchers," after all, especially after being so long away from her. In the morning, the time was more appropriate. I guess she felt guilty, as her opening subject was:

"I am now in charge of the candy and cookie department, and I guess I have been sampling too many of the loose chocolates."

"The extra weight does not look good on you," I said, end of subject.

I never ever saw her at that weight again! We had less than two weeks together, but we filled each and every day. As I remember the weather was extra nice for England, the east coast was a lovely spot when the weather was good.

I seemed to feel a little something different in our relationship, nothing I could put my finger on, but there was something. I had asked her if she had been faithful to me, she said that she had. I was not completely convinced.

I left Langar on the return trip, knowing I had little less than three months remaining in this land of endless, Sand dunes and Dung Beetles.

CHAPTER 29

Return Journey

My last three months in Egypt was served at Rafah, I had hoped to land Charm El Sheik on the Golf of Aquaba. This was the "Piece de Resistance," of the postings, situated on the Southern most tip of the Sinai, close to the Red Sea.

This is the spot where the Diplomats took their secretaries, so they could;

"Take down anything that should come up during the night," if could you catch my drift. It is now a major tourist area for the Israeli populace, and is a Mecca for foreign tourists, a far cry from El Queseima.

At least I was kept busy when working, this was our communication connection back to Canada, and also for all the United Nations offices in the organization, so the traffic was heavy. Also, there were more facilities for entertainment, even snooker hall.

I do sometimes frequent the mess for a beer, as both my friends who had gone on the trips with me, were stationed here, but the noise level, was always two octaves above normal, this, combined with thick tobacco smoke is not my cup of tea.

The movies also were a pleasant change. We also had a visit from

Tommy Hunter of the CBC with his troop. The dancers were met with loud applause at each and every high kick in their routine, as you can well imagine.

The two things we looked forward to most during this period, was the date of our return to Canada. This sometimes was met with bitterness and fisticuffs, when someone found out, that another member was returning earlier than he was, and he had been in Egypt longer. The other was, where we were going to be posted to on our return home to Canada.

I drew Edmonton, so at last I was going out West! My return home was a little different from the remainder of the troops. As my wife was already in England, I had requested that I be allowed to accompany her home. To my mind and thinking, they would allow her to join me on the plane at Langar, and proceed to Canada with the normal rotation.

The minds of the military sometimes do not do what is natural, normal, or common sense, and I was informed that;

"Certainly, you can go back with your wife, but you must pay your own way."

If that was the way they wanted to play, so be it, I was dropped off at Langer with the date that I had to report for duty in Edmonton.

Iris met me at the Langar airport, and we journeyed down to her home. She had already booked passage on the "Empress of Canada," from Tilbury to St. John New Brunswick.

The day I left, I was further informed that I was expected to pay my fare all the way to Edmonton, I had honestly thought they would pick up the tab from St. John to the west. In addition, they informed me that my furniture and effects were in Moncton, New Brunswick and it was my responsibility to arrange, and pay, for them to be transported to Edmonton.

ALBERT M. SWASH

Disappointed at this news, as it would be quite costly for us, my consolation was I would be with my wife, so, that cancelled out the bad news for me, also the money factor from the equation. We arrived in St. John on a cold wet day, we drove up to Sussex, where I had stored that infamous Chevrolet.

We went to another dealer, and purchased a Vauxhall Cresta. I had been very careful with my money, and managed to have a little more money than we were used to having. We immediately set off for Alberta, and, as it was late in November, this is not the time of the year to be travelling such a long distance.

We encountered every type of weather you could imagine, when driving through the eastern provinces, and our progress was relatively slow. After crossing into Michigan, we began to get better weather. On arriving in Minnesota, the roads were dry and flat, as it is on the Prairies. I proceeded to make up a little of our lost time, and then, when cruising along, enjoying being together, the sound of a police siren broke our reverie.

I pulled over, and this State Trooper came up, asking me, to get out of the car and accompany him to his cruiser. Sitting in the passenger seat, I was fascinated by his enlarged dashboard, it had more communication equipment than a detachment in the United Nations.

I received a lecture from this Officer, he asked me of course, where I had come from, and where I was going to, he included Iris in his speech by saying:

"You would not like to have your wife injured, or worse killed, on account of your speeding and driving."

He gave me a cautionary ticket, and said:

"I patrol from here to the Manitoba border, don't let me catch you again."

His approach was much better than if he had given me a proper ticket, he had made me feel foolish, where a ticket would've made me madder than hell, and not achieved half as much.

He did indeed look for us, as shortly after coming into a small town, I took a wrong turn, realizing what I had done, I turned around, and as we returned to the main road he was approaching from the other direction, we were certain he was looking for us.

That evening, as we got on the outskirts of Winnipeg, we stopped at a restaurant with a really Western motif, animal heads on the wall, waitresses in cowboy boots (or is that cowgirl boots?) of course the menu was steaks, and they were delicious.

We finally arrived in Edmonton, four days before Christmas, the temperature was fifty below zero in the wind-chill, we had never been so cold in our lives. It had been one hundred and twenty the day I left El Arish, just a few days ago, so this was some change. Welcome to the West you guys. We were soon shown our first lesson of winter in Alberta.

A fellow traveller, accustomed to the problem we were facing, took out his lighter and carefully placed the flame around the keyhole. When he had succeeded in this endeavor, he informed us to purchase frost shields for the outside of our windows. He then drew our attention to the surrounding cars, to see they were all similarly equipped.

We finally got on our way to the barracks on the outskirts of the city, I found the pay office and prepared to load up like a "Brinks truck." Nothing could have been further from the truth,

"We have no Swash on our payroll list, are you certain you were posted here, the pay clerk asked me.? "Come back in the new year," he added.

I then asked:

97

"I am down to my last few dollars, can I have an advance?"

"I would like to help you, but you are not on the strength of any units here in Edmonton, so there is no way I can advance you any cash."

CHAPTER 30

Christmas

It had been almost 7 weeks since I had left Egypt, and my travel expenses were down to about $50. Not to worry! I had two months back pay in Canada, it was just a matter of checking into the pay office, and sign my name on the pay list! if only it had been that easy!

We left our motel in good time, however, this was Edmonton in December, our little car was frozen solid, and I could not get the key in the lock, to even open the door. We were soon shown our first lesson of winter in Alberta.

A fellow traveller, accustomed to the problem we were facing, took out his lighter and carefully placed the flame around the keyhole. When he had succeeded in this endeavor, he informed us to purchase frost shields for the outside of our windows. He then drew our attention to the surrounding cars, to see they were all similarly equipped.

We finally got on our way to the barracks on the outskirts of the city, I found the pay office and prepared to load up like a "Brinks truck." Nothing could have been further from the truth,

"We have no Swash on our payroll list, are you certain you were posted here, the pay clerk asked me.? "Come back in the new year," he added.

I then asked:

"I am down to my last few dollars, can I have an advance?"

"I would like to help you, but you are not on the strength of any units here in Edmonton, so there is no way I can advance you any cash."

I think that is why we had managed to stay together so long, we seemed to be always in a position where we had to, suck it up, and make do. The motel unit we were staying in, had kitchen facilities, but to make them available to us, we had to pay in advance for another week.

We had no option but to put ourselves at the owner's mercy and explain our position, trusting him believing in us. It was Christmas, and we did not want to hear those words of long ago "there is no room at the inn." They had no stable in the back of this place for us.

He was either a good Joe, or my wife's big brown eyes that did the trick, whatever it was, he let us stay. Not to be daunted we went down to the nearest Dominion store to check out the meat counter, to see what they had on hand, that would fit into our dwindling budget.

We had to settle on a duck, which must have been on a starvation diet, as it barely had enough meat on it for the two of us.

With the aid of some potatoes and Brussels sprouts, and a bottle of cheap port we made do. How can I remember that? believe you me, it is easy, for occasions like that, stick in your mind forever.

The new year came and went, with still no cash available from the pay office. They still insisted that they had not heard of me, and even showing them, my posting instructions made no difference whatsoever. A quick call to the pay office from my Commanding

Officer, however, quickly opened up my account. It is amazing what rank can do.!

We obtained accommodation in a lovely new apartment, our time allowed by the Army for living in a motel, had expired. The trouble was, our furniture had not arrived, and we were living in an empty suite, sleeping on the floor, with bedding that had been lent to us by my comrades.

The arrival time for our furniture was well overdue, so I demanded that my unit send out a tracer to locate it. As it happened, I was just in time, as it had been sent to Calgary, and was about to be shipped back to Moncton in New Brunswick.

Iris obtained a position at the Dominion store from where we bought the duck, turned out to be a great place for her. She rose to be head cashier, and then became the training supervisor for the four new stores the company was building in Edmonton.

I settled in at work, and we were enjoying the comfort and company of each other, leaving yet another minor crisis in our lives behind us.

Almost a year later, I was on the move again, having been selected to go to Kingston in Ontario on a cryptography course. This meant a seven-week separation, which seemed nothing compared with a year in Egypt. The course I was attending was very "hush hush" and it is often said:

"Cryptography, was so secret, the people in it did not know what they were doing."

That was a rumour was put around to stop people asking questions."

We only stayed in Edmonton for four months, before being told that I was moving to Wainwright, still in Alberta, on yet another posting. This was hard for my wife to take, as she was doing so well, and receiving good pay. That, I'm afraid, is a price to pay for being a service man's wife, just another thing to put a strain on the marriage.

The only thing that disturbed me, was the fact, that, my wife had received so many promotions in such a short time. This was further emphasized when she told me that they had a new manager, and he and her were not getting along. It was evident I had still not really got over the first betrayal and was still suspicious.

On hearing of my trip to Wainwright, I requested an interview with the Regimental Sergeant Major, to explain my position, which was that I desperately needed attention on my teeth. I thought he would let me come up from Wainwright (100 miles) for the appointments, even if I had to do it in my own time.

If I had expected any sympathy or help from him, this was quickly dashed. His only comment being:

"You are going to Wainwright to type messages not chew them."
Interview over.!

It would turn out to be another 18 months before the great turn around in my life would finally come to pass.

CHAPTER 31

Warp Time

As I said previously, Wainwright is only about one hundred miles from Edmonton, and except for the first two months we were there, it was like living in a different world. The term "laid-back" must have originated in this community.

The biggest excitement, was on a Saturday evening, when everyone gathered to see the "Iron Horse" as the Canadian National Railway train pulled in. Later that night, you could always witness the weekly punch up outside the Railway Hotel. Oh, I forgot, the annual Rodeo.

The first two months for me however, were hectic, as Camp Wainwright hosts the summer training ground, for all the regular soldiers, and the Militia. They descend from all parts of Canada, and other countries, so the camp is completely transformed.

Even strange ladies appear, to take up residence on a temporary basis, the business was always good, As I was the only cryptographer on staff, it meant I was on call, and seldom a night went past, that I was not called back to camp.

Iris was pretty bored too, so when an opening came up in the Simpson catalogue office, she was only too pleased to start work. A couple had to be very compatible to exist in a relationship, when there is nothing to do. Even television was not available, as the largest antenna could not bring it in from Edmonton.

As the last truck pulled out after the two months of training, the camp returned to being home, as the camp was referred to, by the skeleton staff. For the next ten months, it was not the place for me. I did not like it, and I was not used to having nothing to do.

My Commanding Officer was an avid golfer, and it helped if you went along with his enthusiasm, by purchasing a set of clubs, and accompanying him to the local links. This was an experience in itself, as the greens were sand instead of grass, each green was equipped with a small iron roller, to assist with the putting.

On arriving on the green, you took this roller and smoothed the sand from your ball to the hole and hoped for the best. When I was fortunate enough to play

Later, on a course with grass greens, I found, for the longest time, I could not adjust my game to the speed of the ball.

Learning to putt on sand is not the way to gain experience. Another amusing, but frustrating part of the game, was to hit a long and straight tee shot, only to watch it bounce, and disappear down a Gopher hole.

We explored the surrounding area, which, in itself, took very little time, so it was easy to see why the locals were moribund, and the feeling was catching. We had one interesting outing; our landlady kept insisting that we take a drive to a nearby (as she described it) town.

She informed us proudly that the world champion rodeo cowboy came from their, and it was a place we should not miss.

One nice day, we decided that we had better keep the peace, and we were for ever grateful that we did, as for many years after, it always brought smiles to our faces, for certainly we had never seen anything like this before, or since.

Czar, was the name of the place. As we drove closer to our destination the paved road disappeared, to became a dirt track. We retraced our steps, to make sure we had taken the right turn off. Yes, we were going in the right direction. We could not believe our eyes, it was as if we had been removed in time, to the age of Wells Fargo.

It was a scene from a western movie. It had only one street, with wooden sidewalks, and small stores on each side. The street itself was wider than you would find in a normal town, it even had a saloon bar, with a balcony outside. We were expecting any minute to see a body come crashing out, and over the top, as in "Shane or Gun Smoke," or even, John Wayne come out and take on the bad guy in black.

The only sign of the present age, was a single gas pump, with the sign hung around it like a necklace on a lady, informing all:

"Gas for cash, open from two PM to four PM daily."

The strange part was there were so few people to be seen, using your imagination, it could have been a ghost town.

On our return, we thanked our landlady for directing us to visit Czar, telling her how much we really enjoyed it, which we did.

Christmas was the one special time for us in Wainwright. The previous year spent living in a motel, with the little duck, and no decorations, had been so alien to us. For Iris, the Christmas season was always so joyous

She enjoyed so much, buying and wrapping parcels, then preparing the extra festive goodies, by making mince pies, short breads, gingerbread's and another very special one, she called her:

"Christmas cookies," knowing they were my favourites.

She also made a large Christmas cake, decorated with icing

and seasonal ornaments, and, of course the traditional Christmas pudding.

The Christmas tree was different, we had always had a live green one, but trees of any nature are rare on the prairies. We were forced to buy an artificial tree. I remember Iris was disappointed when I took it out of the box, it did look so ersatz, I must agree.

It was always my job to decorate, so I proceeded with the coloured balls and the lights, then finished it off with tinsel wound around. It was traditional with us that she remained at arm's length during this procedure.

After switching the lights on, I called her in to hear her comments. Her face was the centre of my concentration, as I had got used to the look of pure happiness she gave off, when she first saw the tree. This year was no different.

On Christmas day, she always found an outfit that was traditional, with fabric with shiny threads running through it. Her lovely brown wavy hair would look extra special, earing's with a holiday motive, just enough colouring on her cheeks to light it up, with a trace of lipstick.

You must forgive me, my screen has just misted up at the thought, even now, all these years later, I still remember. "Silent Night, Holy Night," what happy memories of the lovely person.

I was never so glad to be told I was posted out of there. As soon as I found out I was going to Ottawa, Ontario, I phoned home immediately. She too, was excited at the thought of rejoining the mainstream of life.

CHAPTER 32

Joy and Despair

As we journeyed across Canada on our way to Ottawa, neither of us dreamed of the impact this posting would have on our lives, mine in particular. The thought of moving to our capital city, had thrilled us from the start.

We had heard all about its beauty, and of the Tulip Festival in the spring, created from bulbs donated by the country of Holland, in gratitude for the gallant Canadians, who had given their lives, to free the Dutch people from the German occupation. We had seen on television, skating on the Rideau Canal in winter, and the grandeur of the Parliament buildings, we had just left the Alberta Badlands behind.

When I reported for duty, I was a little overwhelmed, to be told I would be working as the cryptographer in the office of the CCOS (Canadian Chief of the Staff Secretariat.) The Official Secrets Act bans me from divulging any more than that.

I can say though, it was a prodigious place to be employed, requiring the highest security clearance, even to be associated with the office. The screening even included my remaining family in England, as well as including our lives prior to us immigrating.

I quickly learned that, if I proved myself, this posting was for as long as I wanted it, as turnovers of the staff, are not advantageous to secrecy.

This feeling of security was welcomed by my better half, as she could now pursue a position with some guarantee, that it would be more permanent. Settling into a nice apartment, we quickly adjusted, and were soon living a happy and contented lifestyle, my wife had obtained a position in Simpson's as a sales clerk, everything looked good

Later she tried out for, and subsequently obtained, a position in the advertising department, a position that led to a more responsible appointment down the line. We had to work around my being on shiftwork, and it was quite usual for me to arrive home, just in time for Iris to drive the car to her workplace.

The overall benefits of being in Ottawa, far outweighed the liabilities, so we were as happy here, as any other place we had lived previously.

However, into each life some rain must fall, and it did here. I had been working in the office for about six months, when one day, upon reporting for work, I was Informed I would be posted to Ellesmere Island for a period of six months.

Do not even look for this on an atlas, as you will never find it, I wish I never had.

As you can well imagine, I was not ecstatic to hear that piece of news, but it was part and parcel of my present employment, as each of us had to take a turn, in this arctic wasteland

Again, I cannot elaborate on this posting, except to say, I never appreciated cold weather, and it doesn't get any colder than up there.

Isolation is another of my least favourite places, but that is life in the Army, you have to take the cards you are dealt with. It is a pity I cannot review some of the happenings in this exotic place.

When the sun does appear, it travels continuously around the horizon, seemingly at a height of only seven or eight feet. That was an experience that I could now add to my resume. Another non-joyous event, regardless of rank, was manually manoeuvring, and then emptying, two hundred-gallon drums of human waste, without spilling a drop.

That is very precarious, to say the least, and difficult to remove, once it is frozen, which it does, in a matter of minutes.

The six-month duty does not exactly fly past. The high point for me was the receipt of mail, and to be thankful, although Iris was working regular hours, she seldom missed a single day of writing to me, we also had the benefit, once again of the Ham radio operator, to help us with our sanity.

There is so much more I could say about that place. I can sum it up in the words of one of my friends, who said:

"They will not get me back here, until they have a car park."

My thoughts exactly.

Nearing the end of my tour, I developed terrible pains in my stomach, severe enough to interfere with my work and sleep, arrangements were then made for me to be airlifted to the USA air base at Thule, in Greenland.

They kept me there for tests for about a week, before contacting Ottawa, to have me evacuated to the hospital down there. A series of tests did not reveal any major problems, and it was put down to my being in a high stress related environment.

If it was, it was not the stress of the work. On the other hand, I would not rule out the separation from my home life as being the cause. Of course, that is mere supposition on my part

Reporting back to the office and resuming the more normal routine of work and play, the pains subsided. How quickly you realize the benefits of regular living after you have been exposed to separation, for even such a short time. The largest benefit of our sojourn in Ottawa is yet to come.

However, my return, did not enhance my fears of indiscretion by my wife. I lived in an apartment block, three stories high, with no numbers on the doors. As I approached my door the first day, I saw a package propped up against my door. I picked it up, it had nothing written on the outside, which was suspicious.

Three hours later, on being joined by my wife, I challenged her with regards to the parcel:

"I have no knowledge of why it would be there," she said,

"You must have some idea of where it came from," I answered.

"There is only one thing I can think of," she replied:

"All the girls have been bothered by this guy in the store, who keeps on hitting on them."

To me, that explained very little, and my greeting was a lot less amorous than it would have been normally. After a while, I regained my composure, and gave her the benefit of the doubt.

Many years later, after she had passed away, it was still bothering me, and I realize now, that I did not ask her the key question.

How did he know which door it was? as the building was multi-storied, and had no identification on the door.?

If there is no afterlife, I will never be able to ask that pertinent question.

CHAPTER 33

Revelation and Reformation

This is the chapter I have been looking forward to writing from the outset, as it contains the happiest time of my life. It was also the first time for another highlight for both of us, I will deal with the latter one first.

We discovered Cape Cod, in Massachusetts, as a place to vacation in our first year in Ottawa, and we journeyed there twice each year and if I have mentioned often, that we could make the most out of our holidays, and we did not have to go to exotic places, or have loads of money, we were happy with the small things of life.

Cape Cod fitted well into this style of life. We had purchased a small boat, a trailer, and a tent for our trips, the boat was loaded to the gunnels with our camping gear. Young, and foolish as we were then, we drove at a ridiculous speed on the New York and Massachusetts Turnpike's, to make the Roland Nickerson State Park in 12 hours, almost to the minute.

Our first visit was for 14 days in early June, when we had the park almost to ourselves. We spent the whole day on the beach, on the Atlantic side of the Cape, fishing for Flounders, which were huge, and known locally as "doormats."

We brown bagged it, buried a few cans of beer in the sand at the water line, to keep it cool, and enjoyed the sun, air, and the fishing. We kept a couple of the fish to barbecue for our evening meal, and released the others for another day.

Nothing could be simpler, to some people I suppose, it would seem boring, not to us, it was everything. We would go back to camp, have our meal, and by 9 o'clock, we were so tired from the fresh air, we would then retire for the night.

I am not ashamed, or embarrassed, to say to make love, how else would two people, who truly love each other act.

The second vacation of the year was in August, and we had quickly learned that the park would be a Mecca to thousands, at that time of the year. This resulted in long lineups waiting for campers to pull out, enabling others to replace them.

This we found was time consuming, so we devised a way around it, not ethical I will admit, but one that got us in a camping spot a lot quicker.

On our earlier trip, we had found a back way into the park, so when we arrived this time, we headed straight for this entrance, drove around until we saw someone vacating, and pitched our tent. When the park warden finally confronted us, if we were not quick enough to get to the registration desk first, we simply told him we were driving around looking for a spot. We then headed to the office and told them our site number. They invariably just asked how we got it. They then shrugged their shoulders and took our money.

We visited Cape Cod again some years later after we moved from Ottawa, it was not the same, the simplicity and the charm of the Cape, had been replaced by greed and avarice.

Now for the Reformation, I think the explanation time is here. I have said on several occasions, "what did Iris ever see in me."

Mary, my friend, and driving force, without whom, I would have abandoned this project, a long time ago, was of the opinion that Iris saw something of the inner me, that is flattering, but suggests of my wife having ESP.

While in Ottawa, I had reason to see an Ear, Nose and Throat Specialist, in the hospital, and, before he asked me what was my complaint, he said:

"Why are you walking around looking like that, you must be laughed at and teased a lot."

I assured him he was quite right; he then went on to say:

"If you want, I can fix your ears and nose, and arrange for a dentist to correct your teeth."

Now you know why I was always grateful for the fact that my wife had overlooked the physical side of me, and had taken a chance.

I entered the hospital, where the surgeon broke and reset my nose, he even took a little off the tip to balance it. My proboscis was packed with cotton batten, so when Iris got in to see me, she must have thought I had just done 10 rounds with Mohammed Ali.

The nose was spread all over my face, my eyes were black, she told me she almost laughed. The doctor then went on to work on my ears, removing some cartilage at the rear, and binding my head up tight in a bandanna.

In two days, I was out of their, with an appointment with the dentist in two weeks time. On my first day out of hospital Iris drove me over to Hull in Québec, and I can still remember, trying to get my fingers inside the head covering, as the pain was so bad, I eventually went in to allow the surgeon to finish the job.

The surgeon was a great guy, and I will always be grateful, that he took the interest in me, to suggest the surgery. He said:

"I would like your wife to be present at the unveiling, she deserves to see the new you."

Iris needed no second bidding; the doctor handed her a mirror to hold while he unwrapped the bandages. As the last one came off, you could hardly see my ears at all, they were pressed so hard against my head. He told us both, that the ears would come out in time to look like everyone else's.

Looking in the mirror I could not believe what was reflected, I looked so different. He then extracted the packing, that sounds a little better than pulled it out.

My nose was straight, my ears were like they should be, and the woman who had loved me when I was certainly not an oil painting, was there to see the transformation. It is now more understandable to you, why I asked myself so often, that question?

My teeth were extracted, and a partial plate made to replace them, I could smile, and look anyone in the face now, and not be subjected to ridicule. Strangely, when I met people again, who had known me before, none made any comment about my new appearance, they would only say that I looked different and younger. How complementary!

CHAPTER 34

On the Move Again

It was the year 1965, and we had been married twenty-eight years, and the "bloom was still on the rose." Ottawa had been very good to us. My promotion to Sgt. along with the new lease on life, afforded me by my cosmetic surgery, resulted in my esteem receiving a boost.

It was no surprise that the end of our third year in Ottawa was nearing. I had let it be known, that I wished to carry on in my present position. Coincidently, the person in charge of the office was retiring from the service, as his end in the service had caught up with him. I had enjoyed an extremely good relationship with this supervisor, and was sorry to see him go. Often changes in command can alter the chemistry of the office. This was such a case for me.

When his replacement was announced, several of the other people who had known the supervisor previously, said that we were lucky to get him, as he was a nice guy. That might very well have been, but his relationship with me, never did get off the ground

I have no idea for his dislike of me, but from the pettiness of his memo's, pinned on the notice board, for all to read, coupled with my working hard, while at the same time, trying not to make a mistake, created a situation where I no longer wanted to go to the office to perform my duties.

In my last few days in the office, I found out that it was my English connection that had disturbed him, as he was a French-Canadian, with an English wife.

In this particular office, and the critical nature of the work being done there, it commanded every ounce of your time and concentration, cooperation and peace of mind were a vital necessity.

Four months after he took over, I requested a posting, it was the first time I had ever done this. The commanding officer called me to his office and reminded me that only three months previously, I had asked to remain in my present position.

"It is a conflict of personalities," I told him.

I informed him, He seems to disagree on everything, I do, and, as he holds the upper hand by the virtue of his rank, it makes it impossible for me."

He was not happy with me, as they did not like to change any personnel, in this particular office, but he agreed finally, that it was not in the interest of anyone, to keep me there unsatisfied.

My wife was not happy with this development, as she was doing very well, and we were beginning to enjoy a better style of life. However, she had seen the change in me, and knew I had given it considerable thought, before I had decided on this path. Fate has been mentioned by me on several occasions, it happened again, with this decision.

Eventually my posting came through, Camp Debert, just outside Truro, Nova Scotia, we were back in the Maritimes again. The work was exactly the same as it was in Edmonton, which meant I was temporarily out of cryptography, and now a supervisor in the communication centre.

The teletype trade had groups one, two, and three, and the third was cryptography. Training wise, I had reached the highest level. Meanwhile, Ottawa had been working on making a new grouping, which was a necessary requirement to become a senior supervisor.

This was the first course of the new grading, it was held in Kingston, Ontario, and it was restricted for Chief Warrant officers only. The second course was to include sergeants, one hundred and fifty of whom were selected from across Canada. They were required to write an extensive test, the top fifteen would attend a seven months course at the School of Signal's in Kingston, Ontario.

I was one of the one hundred and fifty, if had I had remained in Ottawa, my name would not have been entered, so fate again played a big part

Our tests were written at our individual stations, as it would be impossible to get all the sergeants in one place. They had a unique way of doing this examination, each participant was allocated a number from a master list in Ottawa, the name never appeared on the test paper.

The names and numbers were then sent to Kingston, where the papers were marked, and here the name and the number were reunited.

When the results came back my CO informed me, that he was very disappointed, as I had only scored fifty seven percent, he did not tell me at that time, that the other two members who had written the test with me, did not receive the required minimum pass.

He was disappointed, I was disgusted.! I had always felt I had a good handle on my trade, that percentage was extremely poor. That night, when I got home, I waited before telling Iris my score, I told her:

"We will not be going to Kingston, I only just managed to pass."

Five weeks later, I was scheduled to attend the group four course at Kingston, as, even with that low score, I had finished seventh overall, the top mark being in the low sixties.

The examination had been set at a very high standard, to ensure only a minimum number would pass. Meanwhile, my wife had made up her mind she was not going to stay in Truro on her own, she was coming with me. We left our boat and trailer behind; the future was now ours to discover.

CHAPTER 35

Living Rough

We arrived in the Gananoque area just outside of Kingston for the second time, leaving us in good time to seek a camping spot. However, the weather was still not really conducive tenting, so we considered ourselves very fortunate to discover a camping site, that had some large RV's, which were rented out in the summer, but now stood empty.

The owner was only too pleased to recover some hard cash during his quiet time. He also owned a general store on the property, so he was not exactly starving. We developed a good rapport with him, and were extremely happy to reside there for a couple of months at least.

On checking into the base, I found my time would be fully taken up on this seven-month course. The curriculum left little time for leisure, as considerable study time was necessary, after the normal day's instruction was completed. This had to be done in the classroom, as the material was not allowed off base, as it was too sensitive.

We decided this would be an ideal time, to invite a niece of Iris's to visit, and stay for the summer break. This arrangement could very well have ended in tragedy.

Many times, since the demise of my wife I have advised all I meet that they must enjoy every minute they are together. Never part for work, or go to sleep, without a kiss, or a loving word. This was a classic example of what might happen.

That day I left for work as normal, kissed my wife and our new acquaintance goodbye, and accepted it as just another day at the office.

The following entry was narrated by my wife. It was a beautiful sunny and warm morning, the two of them basked in the sun's rays, as both were sun worshipers.

The store owner said to them:

"You should go over to that island in your boat, there are lots of wild strawberries you can pick." The island was well within a rowing distance, as it was only about three quarters of a mile from the RV, Iris, who was normally scared of the water, decided to make the trip as it was calm and inviting. The trip over was uneventful, and with an oar each, they had no difficulty rowing to their destination. They took a picnic lunch, and pails for the berries, that they were going to collect, and it was an exciting trip for them.

On arriving, they picked, talked, and laughed together, however, they failed to see the ominous black clouds fast approaching them. Their first notification of danger was the sudden feel of a strong wind, followed by heavy rain, thunder. and lightning

They should have remained on the island, subjected to, of course, the risk of a lightning bolt, the alternative decision they took turned out being far more dangerous. After the event, my wife realized this, but her immediate worry was for her young niece who was only fifteen years old at the time.

They rushed for the boat, Iris took both oars, and they set out for home. She soon realized, that she was making no progress, regardless of how hard she rowed. The water was breaking over the bow, and aided by the heavy rain, the boat was soon taking on water very fast. With nothing to use to bale the water out, things were getting desperate.

Fate was with them. The store owner knew they had gone out, so he checked with his binoculars, realizing their difficulty, he set out in his larger boat to rescue them from their peril.

He got the small boat on his lee side, then assisted the girls to scramble aboard. Securing the small boat to the stern of his larger vessel, he returned them to his jetty. I had been conscious of the storm as it passed over the camp, I knew it had gone in the general direction of my family, but I never realized they were in such grave danger.

It was close to nine in the evening before I returned to the camp, both girls were still visibly disturbed. There was no way that Iris would go out on such a venture again. What if they had succumbed on that day, and I had left for work in an angered state, imagine the additional pain I would have had to live with.

As June the first drew close, we had to find new accommodation for both of them. We moved several miles nearer to the camp, set up our tent and another for my Niece, (another Iris,) as she had been named after her aunt. It was a nice spot by the water.

The girls got lots of swimming and sunbathing. When they wanted to go shopping, my wife drove me to work and picked me up, it was not exactly rough living. The younger Iris had to leave for Nova Scotia in August, this meant my Iris was on her own, on a deserted campsite, as she was the lone tenant, as the tourist season was over.

My course ended in the third week in September. The camping was getting decidedly cool by this time. Iris was noticeably disgruntled the night I had my graduation dinner, as no guests were allowed.

Incidentally, I was the only course member who had his dependent with him.

I dined on Fillet Mignon while she had a tin of baked beans (that is how she told her story anyway.) Following the party, the instructor invited some of us to his house. He gave me time to pick up my love, and I took her with me. So, all was not lost.

The next morning, we packed up for our return to Truro. We had succeeded in being together as much as possible, and once again she had made the sacrifice for me. I was now an official Group 4, having successfully passed the course, so everything looked like the possibility of another posting coming up, I wonder.?

CHAPTER 36

Awareness

I have made frequent references to the coincidences and fate throughout this narrative, it is only because on reliving our story, I am amazed how often they occurred to influence our life together. Yet another was in the offing.

My return to camp Debert caused a dilemma for the powers to be, I was junior in rank to every shift supervisor, but senior in the teletype trade. The commanding officer gave me a desk in the communication centre, with no terms of reference. It was not a happy situation.

On my recent course, the only subject to which I did not meet the required standard, was my writing. For the first time in my life I was marked as holding up the rest of the class (15th out of 15.) With that in mind, imagine my surprise that the Captain, who had been my course officer at Kingston, had been promoted to the rank of Major, to replace my CO, here in Debert.

I make this point, as his first designated job for me, was to start a Newspaper. You can well imagine, I felt like reminding him of his recent opinion of my journalistic capabilities, but one is not in a position to do that in the Armed Forces.

Iris thought this development was hilarious:

"I want to see the first issue." she said, laughing hysterically.

"What on earth are you going to write about?" she had a valid point.

"Maybe you can use your sense of humour and include a fictitious Dear Abby item" She was really enjoying my new predicament.

"From out of the mouth of babes," she had given me an idea, should I give her credit.? Not yet, I decided quickly.

My boss, of course, was doing this to get the other Senior NCOs off of his back for complaining about me being junior in rank to them. He was not just giving me something to do to pass the time, he wanted to keep them at bay.

He had suggested that I make this a monthly addition of the camp newspaper, this was the only suggestion he gave me, and I was on my own. Some recent incidents at a dance in the Sgt.'s mess gave me a license to exaggerate some of the happenings around camp, by adding some humour, and some activities in the various messes, gave me more material.

The paper began filling in some space. Now, remembering Iris's Dear Abby suggestion, I started using segments of what I heard the guys talking about, thus bringing them into it without naming names.

Her reaction as she read it, was pleasing for me to see the odd smile appeared as she read the pages. Looking up she said,

"I never thought you would pull it off, I think they will like it." Praise indeed, for she seldom let loose with compliments to me.

My wife had always been a very healthy person, but she suddenly got very sick. She had been complaining of stomach pains for some time, I had got her to the doctor, but he dismissed it as not serious.

One night, she was in real pain, so I rushed her to the emergency department.

They admitted her, and the next day she had an operation on her gallbladder,

In those days, they made a large incision, not the three small holes that they do today. I remember going into her room in the afternoon, it was the first time I had seen a person in post operation.

She lay there looking like death was just around the corner, her face was white, her eyes shut. I had to look close at her to be sure she was breathing, I kissed her, she did not move, I was scared, the nurse assured me everything was alright, so I left the room, with much less confidence than the nurse.

When I returned in the evening she was sitting up, she had a trace of lipstick, with a little blush on her cheeks, and was smiling from ear to ear. It was my first experience, but it was not to be my last.

My journalistic achievements did not last for very long however. On my recent course, I had developed a desire to be an instructor, and had gotten the best marks for that portion of the course.

One of the teaching requirements of the course had been humorous, if not a little scary. A list of seemingly stupid objects was placed in a box from which we each picked one. We then had to give a forty-minute lecture on our resulting pick, or, as long as we could manage.

I drew a cup and saucer, and I fantasized for the required amount of time, which even included a few minutes on the "Mad Hatter's tea party," to fill out my diatribe. I liked the challenge, and realized the idea of teaching appealed to me.

It was not always the practice of Army Headquarters to pay special interest to anyone who requested a particular function to perform. Often misfits were introduced to key positions, in this instance, such was the case.

They had posted a Sgt to the school as an instructor, who did not have the aptitude to teach, did not want to be there, and was thoroughly miserable in his position. It was my good fortune to cross post with him. Once more, we were on the move.

This time it was back to Kingston, to the place that had caused me so much misery at the outset of my military career, this time however, I was in the position of dishing it out. I had learned one huge lesson from the previous visit, it was better to pass on knowledge, than ridicule people, I vowed not to fall into the latter category.

Iris was excited at the thought of moving. She liked Kingston, and felt she had a chance to resume her career with the Sears store in the advertising department, where she had gained experience while she was in Ottawa. As it turned out, she obtained a position right away, as assistant to the advertising manager. So, we were both on cloud nine.

One of the benefits Iris especially enjoyed by working at Sears was the availability of clothes being close at hand. She was very dress coordinated, as I said before, and it soon became customary for the manager of the dress department to ring her up, to inform her that a new shipment had arrived.

I swear she returned half of the stipend she earned each month, from whence it came. In fairness to her, she did not dress to show off, she had a genuine love to look nice, and she felt good when dressed attractively. I never argued with her over this, why should I? I noticed the looks she received whenever we went out, they could only look, it was my arm she was holding.

CHAPTER 37

Satisfaction all Round

We had purchased a 14 x 62 mobile home a few months before we left Truro, so our immediate consideration was getting it placed in the vicinity of Kingston. The province of Ontario had some of the most restrictive laws for these types of homes, and this placement became no easy task, finally we were able to find a pad in a trailer court near Collins Bay penitentiary.

The owner should have been in the penitentiary, not alongside it, as he had a monopoly, and well he knew it. Soon after we set up, our water froze throughout the camp. He assembled all of us trailer owners, supplied us with hoses to fix on our car exhaust pipes, and then ordered us to start our engines, and direct the hoses down the conduits containing the water lines.

We had no option but to carry out this crazy man's plans. It was obvious by him having his stock of hoses, that this problem had occurred previously. We finally succeeded in regaining our water supply

Upon re-entering our mobile home, the carbon dioxide fumes had come up from the underground conduits, although they were supposed to be odourless, we were fully conscious of them. Iris was concerned for our neighbour, a young man who worked the night shift.

We went to his place to try to awaken him with out any success, fortunately, he had left his door unlocked, allowing us to half carry, and drag him outside, where he immediately threw up, and was in great distress. A few minutes longer, and he would have been deceased.

This episode forced us to move a considerable distance out from the city to Deseronto. It was a nice park, situated on Lake Ontario, a delightful spot in the summer, but not in the winter. On one occasion, I was home on a day off, while unfortunately, Iris had to go into work.

During the morning a heavy snowstorm developed, so all I could do was sit and wait, as she had our car. There was no way I could get into town to assist her, the clock ticked on, I became more and more agitated. The radio was informing everyone to keep off the highway, so, as I had not received any phone calls from her, I had hoped that she would have made arrangements to stay in Kingston. I was nearly a basket case with worry, eventually she did arrive home, but it had taken her several hours to make it, the roads were in such treacherous conditions, and they had caused a serious accident, thankfully, not to her, this had further held her up

She was relieved to have gotten home safely, I was equally relieved. I do not know who was the most distressed. We looked around for a more suitable site, and once again, we found ourselves in Gananoque.

As for our other life, it was progressing exceedingly well. My wife had secured the position of advertising manager and was making the most money she had ever made, which was incidentally, only seventy percent of her male predecessor. Meanwhile I was very happy and secure in my position, which was both challenging and rewarding.

Remember that Cpl, the one who insulted my wife, by referring her as my mother. Do you recall I had made him my personal enemy, and placed him on my list for future consideration.? Well, a week or so before a new course arrives for training, we receive the nominal role, of the incoming students.

It was common practice to scan the names, to see if there were any, we had previous dealings with. The reason for this was twofold, one out of interest, the other to localize any malcontents who might disrupt the other members of the course.

There was his name, Cpl. P, was it the same one.? If so, he had proved that my assessment of him as having a low IQ, was correct. He was still a Cpl., I had not only caught up with him in rank, I had passed him.

How would I react? That night, when I informed Iris of his pending arrival, I must have passed on the exhilarated feeling I had for possible revenge:

"Be yourself," she said, "do not change your principles for self gratification," that was food for thought.

The first day of this class arrived, I entered the lecture room, took my place at the rostrum, casually glancing at their faces until I saw him sitting near the back.

I have no idea of his reaction on seeing me, he had probably found out ahead of time, that I would be his instructor. He knew well enough that I had the power to give him a RTU (return to unit) with no questions asked by my superiors, however, my mind was made up on how my treatment for him would be.

I addressed the class as I did for all my classes:

"My name is Sgt. Swash, I am your instructor, I will attempt to teach you as much as I can. I will expect you to absorb as much, as your brains will allow. Your marks will be what you earn, you will not be given any pre-examination tips, of what the possible final exam questions might be. Finally, you all have an equal opportunity to succeed or fail. I know some of you from the past, which will have no bearing on the outcome. It is up to you. Any questions?"

Another character of my basic training days was the Sgt. Major, who rehearsed his drill in front of the mirror, remember him.? He was now the head non-commissioned officer in the school, as such, the sergeants mess was his private domain.

It was protocol, I found this out too late, that on your first visit to the mess with your spouse, your first responsibility is to introduce her to him Even before you partake of any beverages, or find a place to park your carcass, you seek him out to pay your respects. The very first time I caught his eye, I realized, I was in deep trouble, however, the evening passed without incident, and we had a good time.

As it was a Saturday evening, I had to wait until Monday morning to receive his wrath. I was interrupted in my first period of the day and informed that the RSM required me to make an appearance in his office, at the first available moment.

You do not treat this tardily, as he knows full well when you are not engaged with students, and he expects you in his office in minutes. I must admit I had trepidation at the thought of meeting him in this situation.

I approached his office, cautiously, I had no wish to further antagonize him.

"Who is it he yelled?

"Sgt. Swash Sir," I replied

"Get in here!" An octave higher.

He decidedly did not sound happy

"You insulted me on Saturday night," he yelled, "You bring your wife and introduce her to me on your first visit to my mess, you understand."

(There was more in his tirade, but young people might be reading this.)

He was having a field day at my expense, eventually, he dismissed me.

I informed Iris of my ordeal, and as far as she was concerned, we needn't go there anymore. We did however, and this time the RSM was so nice to my wife, I couldn't believe it was in him. As he dismissed us, he said, just loud enough for me to hear "That's more like it." On a later date, he informed me that I had a very nice wife, you see, he was human.

CHAPTER 38

Too Settled

We underwent a period in the next three years, where we were settled into our environment, a steady routine of time off. Identical living patterns between us for the first time. I was dropped off at Vimy each working day, and then Iris proceeded to Sears for her daily grind. At four thirty pm, I got a lift from the school to the mall where the store was situated. We were as financially secure, as at any time in our marriage, however, it appeared we had lost the ability to enjoy the small mercies in life.

The only vacation we had at this time was to Expo 1967 in Montréal. We could have driven direct from Gananoque, but my wife's brother in Nova Scotia, thought it would be a good idea, if we took two of his teenagers and their friends with us.

We had a tent trailer that we could use, as the kids had their own tents. It would be necessary for us to drive to Dartmouth N.S. to pick them up. We drove through the USA, enjoying a few days in New Hampshire, Vermont and Maine, again, before re-entering Canada.

We had never had our own family, but twelve days with those four, and we were not sorry that wasn't the case. All four were young teenagers, without a single care, or responsibility between them. They were ever ready for meals, but always had some project that must be done right away, when the dishes and the cleanup came around.

The boys were continually teasing the girls, who in turn spent more time primping and preening, than anything else. Iris tried so hard to make things good for them, but those good intentions came for naught, we hoped that when we got to expo things would improve.

The moment we entered the Expo grounds, it became obvious that things would not be the way we wanted them. Arranging for them to meet us for lunch at a specific time, outside of one of the pavilions, they immediately ran off in different directions.

In due course, they all arrived for lunch, their stomachs full of junk food, that they had been eating all morning. The nice basket of fruit and food, we had been toting around all that time, turned out to be just for us. The afternoon had us carrying the basket, interfering with our enjoyment, while they were free and wild, to go as they pleased.

The next morning, we had a change of plans, I informed them that they were on their own, if they wanted food, they could procure it in the same way they had the previous day. This did not faze them one little bit, but it did allow us to take our time, and enjoy what Expo had to offer.

The return trip was more of the same, it was with the greatest of pleasure that we turned them over to their parents. Not a single "Thank You" from the young hellions. A few more days of peace and tranquility on the return half of the journey, a good bed and shower in a motel, this was much better than the tent.

My partner was under a more stressful environment than I. She had a strict quota of space available to her for the store promotions. Each manager wanted his, or, her department be given the maximum exposure, consequently, she was cajoled, flattered, sweet talked and then sometimes accused of favouritism, while always being answerable to a difficult, and hard to please, store manager.

There were times when this frustration came home with her, interfering with our relationship. There was another moment of doubt, that crept into my life. One day, I knew that I would finish early in camp, so I arranged to get picked up, earlier than normal.

Consequently, I was early getting to the store. On entering, I immediately noticed that Iris was in a deep conversation with someone, who was much too close to her for my liking.

Immediately on seeing me, they separated very quickly, and suspiciously. I did not say anything at the time, but I was far from happy. Of course, later, when I brought up the subject while driving home, she had an excuse. This is yet another time I had to listen to some dubious excuses.

Adding salt to the wounds, I had to travel to Ottawa for a couple of weeks, immediately following this confrontation. I had been selected from Ottawa, to write the training specifications for the teletype and cryptography trade, with a warrant officer from the Air Force in that city.

This meant I would be away from Monday to Friday, and it came up too quickly following the close proximity problem we were just getting over. I know if I had my car, I would have dropped in on one of those days. I did not like living like this.

This added responsibility could have been taken as a vote of confidence in my ability, anyway, the finished version was accepted in its entirety, and typical of the Army we never received even a thanks you for a job well done. I did not know at the time, but recompense was in the offing.

After three years of satisfying employment, doing something but

I really liked, but my time in Kingston was coming to an end. I had absolutely no idea of this, until one morning, during a break between classes I was called to the COs office. Have you noticed how often it always comes to me from out of the blue.?

My commanding officer was on exchange from the British Signal Corps, and it had been a pleasure to work for him:

"Sgt." he said, "I have some good news, and some bad news for you, the bad news is, I am going to lose you, During your employment in this squadron we have been extremely happy with your work, and we are extremely sorry to see you go" he paused,

"The good news is, you have been promoted to Warrant Officer and posted to Germany with the United Nations."

He waited to see my reaction, as his announcement had come completely as a surprise, and it took a few moments for it to sink in.

I was genuinely sorry to be leaving. I knew that the project I had been instrumental in planning, while serving here, would remain as long as the teletype trade was in operation.

"I am sorry to be leaving the school and instructing here, I have really enjoyed my stay," I told him.

It was even tempting for me to turn down the promotion, but after three years, a move for me was imminent, so I will move on. He then invited my wife and I to join him, and his wife for supper a few nights later. Little things like that make you feel appreciated. So different to be told this, in the same school, that I had been subjected to verbal abuse so many years previously:

"This man does not have the necessary requirements to ever be considered for promotion." Comes to mind.

I hesitated a while before I informed Iris, I thought she would be very happy to go, as her mother was still alive in England. She also had a sister there. I knew she was at times frustrated with her position at Sears, but she took a lot of pride in being capable in her capacity there.

Finally, I broached the subject and she was delighted. She informed me for the first time that she was tired of being harassed by one and then another, and that she welcomed the opportunity to go to Europe, as she said:

"To open another chapter in our lives."

As it turned out, that was the last position in the working world that she would hold.

CHAPTER 39

Oktoberfest and Sauerkraut

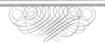

The next few weeks were hectic, we had decided to sell our mobile home, and its contents, to make a fresh start when we returned to Canada. Our posting was for three years, which was a longer time, than I had remaining in the military. I had another two years and a few months, then I would be returning to civilian life.

Both of us had warmed at the prospect of living and touring around Europe. My only concern was, the last time I had any dealings with Germans, I was fighting them. The intervening years had done nothing to ease my opinion of them. I realized, that in my new position I would be working alongside them as a member of NATO.

We left Trenton Ontario on a Canadian Armed Forces Boeing 707, my flying fears had improved considerably, I could now unclench my fists at 36,000 feet, and listen intently for any unusual noises, then pray loudly whenever the airplane banked. I no longer looked out for angels in the clouds, as they are depicted in paintings of heaven.

I still was not the consummate flyer; however, my fears were certainly put to the test as we approached Düsseldorf airport for landing. Our pilot definitely did not help my cause, when he announced that the airport was socked in with thick fog.

The aircraft was bucking like a rodeo stallion, I felt the hydraulic bump, as the wheels were lowered, my eyes were glued to the window, looking for some sight of land. Row upon row of houses suddenly appeared only seconds before we touched down on the runway, the terminal was a welcome sight.

We were not allowed to take our cat on a service aircraft, so she was put on an Air Canada flight, to be picked up by us at Düsseldorf. When we arrived, the cat was not there, so the attendant telephoned around, only to find out she was in Berlin, so we had to wait and pick her up the next day.

We were picked up and transported to Wickrath, a small town about five miles from the camp at Rheindahlan, where the British married quarters were situated. We were allocated a second-floor apartment in the Senior NCO's block.

I prepared myself to be "marched in," and as we had no children, we had never previously qualified in Canada for married quarter accommodation, so this marching in ceremony was new to us.

Iris was not happy, having to sit in the car while I entered to check the inventory and sign for the contents. The housing officer read me the riot act, then he left, and Iris and I were allowed in.

The apartment had two bedrooms, with a large living room, a kitchen and a full bathroom. It was fully furnished with heavy German furniture.

The floors were black tiles throughout, shined so brightly, you could almost see your reflection in them. A few scatter rugs were in evidence, purchased previously, and then left behind by former tenants. The accommodation was very comfortable, and we quickly made ourselves at home.

The working arrangements for me were different to any I had experienced previously. We worked three-day shifts, of 12 hours on, and 12 hours off. The main difference was, we left Germany to work in Holland, and were billeted in Belgium when off duty, confusing to you.?

When in were billeted in Belgium, we worked in deep caves at Maastricht in Holland. During the war this location had been used by the Jews as a refuge, and there were many etchings scratched in the walls to bear this out.

Before going down for my first tour of duty, I had to attend a one-week familiarization course with the British Army. This consisted of general information on what was expected from us, regarding our relationship with the German civilians.

Also, we received warnings about the dangerous driving conditions on the autobahn, as there were no speed limits, and one hundred and twenty km an hour was a common speed. I quickly learned that an accident involving ten or twenty cars, was considered a fender bender.

A short course on the German language was included, which I found very difficult. One amusing anecdote came from this however, which I will try to narrate.

The instructor told us we should practice a sentence that we could use on the economy (the term used for living out of camp.)

"You Canadians" he said, "all own cars, so I suggest you learn the following sentence":

"Geben sie mier bitte fumpcene liter benzine." I practised this diligently, until it was time to fill up with gasoline. The attendant came out, and I pumped out my chest, and called out the German equivalent of:

"Give me please, 15 litres of gasoline."

He gave me a cursory look, then with a thick Cockney accent, (English) he said:

"Wait a minute mate, I will get a Kraut, I don't speak Deutsch." True story, he turned out to be a British soldier moonlighting for extra Deutsch marks. How about that for lowering your ego.

One very helpful piece of information was given, this was with reference to travel. The instructor recommended we purchase a used Caravan (English for a RV) he went on to say:

"When you trade it in, you will lose very little,"

I took his advice and was very glad that I did. We travelled extensively for two of the three years I was over there. Visiting Holland, Belgium, Luxembourg, Austria, Switzerland and Spain, the latter place where we enjoyed a special three weeks on the Costa Bravo on the Spanish coast.

We camped most weekends when we were not on long journeys at a campsite on the Rhine at Lauralie Rock, a famous landmark. The owner of this spa, looked like an identical twin of Shultzy in "Hogan's heroes," the TV sitcom of yesteryear, we quickly became friends, he called me his Canadian friend:

"You teach me English, I teach you Deutsch," was his greeting every time we met, and regardless of how many other campers he was turning away, when his camp was full, he always had room for us.

I was not very happy at this time, with one aspect of my career. The forces do it like the trade union's do, with their last in first out policy. The military adopts a policy of a seniority list, once you get on it, it is just a matter of time that you have to wait for promotion, regardless of your ability. I knew that the Warrant Officer immediately above me, had been promoted to Master Warrant Officer, so any day I should have received my next promotion.

I then began to find out the reason why I had not received my promotion, it appeared that other junior Warrant Officers to me, were being promoted to the higher rank. Later, I was to find out the reason for this was Paul Hellyer, the Liberal Minister of Defence, had changed the existing policy, by lowering the retirement age to fifty, instead of fifty-two, which meant that personnel like myself, who, if moved up in rank, would not be allowed to serve until that age.

He ordered that these candidates names would be asterisked, with a notation taken, not to be promoted. I mentioned this, as later you will discover, that fate, had yet again, entered our lives.

CHAPTER 40

Clinical Poisoning

A few trips down to the caves on my own, were enough for Iris to decide this three-day separation was not for her. She wanted no part of sitting around for days, waiting for me to come home:

"Next time you are down there," she said "look for a camp ground, I will be happier in Tongeron with you."

It did not come as any surprise to me, as whenever, or where ever, we had been together, as long as work had not interfered, she would make a point of us being in each other's company. Of all the fifty-five Canadians on the post, we were the only couple who took advantage of this arrangement.

Ten months after arriving in Germany, Iris began to feel sick. She found it necessary to visit the British military hospital in Rheindahlen for a checkup. Following several tests, she was admitted, and placed in quarantine, with a diagnosis of TB of the Uterus. They released her after a few weeks, but her condition gradually worsened. The doctors had prescribed the drug Streptomycin and it was pitiful to watch her, as she tried to live a normal life.

At the same time, we got another surprise, the Canadian government had decided to close down the detachment in Rheindahlen and by so doing returned most of the personnel to Canada. We had never thought we would get another posting before returning home. The three personnel who had arrived in Germany with me, were the only members to remain.

The four of us were moved to Baden Solignen in southern Germany, close to the world-renowned spa "Baden-Baden. Iris made the journey with great difficulty, as her condition had deteriorated to the point where she had no balance whatsoever, and she was walking into the furniture and reeling from wall to wall. It was heartbreaking for me to see her in such a state.

On arriving at the hospital in Lahr they instantly placed her in the Intensive Care Unit. The first action they performed was to take her off the medication, which was the chief culprit for her condition, Iris was literally being poisoned to death.

After several weeks of tests, it was discovered she did not have TB, but Fibroids. These were removed as soon as she was able to have surgery. With the combination of the withdrawal of the drugs, accompanied by two months of rest and relaxation, she gradually returned to near pre-illness. In addition, this had interrupted our planned vacation to Italy for that year.

Her recovery was helped by us having short trips to nearby France, which was only 3 miles from our apartment in Germany, and to the South, it was just a two-hour drive to Switzerland.

I had my first introduction to escargot and frog legs while I was there. The Commanding Officer had arranged for the monthly staff meeting to be held in a restaurant just over the Rhine River in France. This was my first meeting in my new position, so, I was a trifle apprehensive, as I was amongst complete strangers.

I watched carefully as my compatriots attacked their entrée. I had been informed on the way over what fare would be served, it almost caused me to throw up at the thought.

Gingerly taking my first bite, I found out if I forgot what I was eating, they were very good. The fun part was when I got home. My wife was already in bed, and as I opened the bedroom door, she asked:

"How did the meeting go?"

"Good," I said

That was enough for her, she hid her head beneath the covers and yelled:

"Sleep in the other room, that garlic is awful."

I was still a good six feet away from her; it must have been powerful.

That summer we took our trailer down to the Costa Sol on the East coast of Spain. This was one of our most enjoyable holidays, and another one that will be long remembered. We travelled down to the Mediterranean coastline of France, which was just beginning to be built up, as a rival to the famous French Riviera.

Try as I might, I could not get my other half to spend one overnight stop at a nude resort on our way down. Looking straight at me, she said:

"I don't want to create a fuss over such a little thing,"

I am sure that was the first complaint I had ever received from her. In any case, I was not serious. I was too jealous to share her with other leering men.

We stayed at Camp Roma for a few days, what a beautiful place. The property rose up from the beach, to a high elevation in a narrow bay, covered with exotic trees and shrubs.

Upon reaching the campsite we had a magnificent view over the water. The beach area was very small, with lovely white sand, swimming was confined to the sheltered bay, with crystal clear warm water, life could not be any better.

The majority of the Canadian Establishment migrated to a campsite near Barcelona called "The laughing whale." Not wanting to be kept out of this trend, we made our way down the coast to Barcelona. On our arrival we were placed in the reserve area, as the site was full.

We were parked close to the water, which was filthy with flotsam. The mosquitoes were in dense hordes, forcing us to close up everything in the caravan that would shut. Then, as we were about to go to sleep, the burr from one of these pesky insects, which seemingly were dedicated on extracting blood from our heads. This caused us to hunt the varmint down, and execute it, we then settled down again for a few minutes, only to have to repeat the procedure.

Our patience was wearing thin, a heated word was now and then exchanged between us, until we discovered where the predators were entering. We had placed a plug in the sink, this had ended their attacks, and allowed us to rest at last. Immediately upon opening her eyes the next morning, Iris said:

"I want to leave here, and return to Roma." I needed no second bidding either.

On our return from this holiday, we arranged for Iris's mother to come over, partly as a holiday for her, and also help in the further recovery of Iris. This arrangement became permanent in a short time, as her mother, also became incapacitated, resulting in her being air evacuated to Norwich in England, by a Canadian aircraft.

On her mother's recovery, my wife continued her short hiatus in England, with the intention of settling her mother's business. On their return, my mother-in-law became part of the immediate family for the next fourteen years.

No mother-in-law jokes are necessary!

CHAPTER 41

Exit the Military

My time in the forces was quickly winding down. We had taken full advantage of our opportunities to travel. It had been an enjoyable period with the obvious exception of the illness to Iris. Fortunately, there did not appear to be any permanent effects from the drug reaction.

My efforts to get some kind of settlement in the way of employment in Canada, were met with frustration. My first choice was British Columbia, but the replies I received from them amounted to; don't come here, unless you already have a position to come to, or plenty of money. So, I had to look elsewhere.

The Canadian government was already engaged in the cutback program as early as 1972. They had decided to turn the message centre in Lahr, over to the German army. So, an opportunity to become the first civilian in this position was offered to me, it would have meant my moving down to Lahr.

We would continue to have the right to use the Canadian PX to purchase groceries etc., and with an honorary membership of the Senior NCOs mess, with permission to travel on the Canadian service aircraft.

There was no time limit on the length of time that I could have that position at Lahr, we gave it serious deliberation, but decided against it. This proved another fortunate twist of fate for us.

The military were pressing me to select my place of residence in Canada, as we were allowed just one paid move on our return. My efforts to obtain employment with the civil service in Canada, where I would be able apply my experience in communications was with the Navy, it appeared at first, to bear fruit. As I received notification that a position would be available to me on my return.

This promise was enough for me to apply to the Army to move my family and effects to the Halifax area. By this time my wife was really looking forward to this rehabilitation. Her mother would be returning with us, this is a where Iris's brother, resided just outside of Dartmouth, so it appeared to be a wise decision on our part.

My departure from the Canadian forces was almost as cold as my entrance, it was referred to, as my "golden handshake, it was anything but that. We landed in Trenton, Ontario, one evening, the very next morning I was processed to be a civilian, without a single "best of luck" or similar well wish. "thanks, but no thanks" was the implication I took with me.

Our conservation in our money matters was costly for us. We had the opportunity of purchasing a new house, in a new subdivision for $27,000. Our fear of making a commitment, with the possible loss of the property by defaulting on the payments, showed our lack of financial acumen.

We chose the route of purchasing a lot and developing it. We had the lot cleared, installed a septic bed, drilled a well etc. We then purchased a large mobile home to place on it. When the dust had settled, we had used up as much capital, as we would have done by purchasing the house.

With decisions like that, it is understandable why we did not accumulate wealth, however, what we had together was far more valuable than material things.

My wife had a sixth sense that the communication position was not set in stone, how right she was. On requesting an interview with the gentleman who had assured me of a position by mail, his response on confronting me was:

"We have not placed anyone in the dockyard communication centre for two years, I do not know who gave you that impression."

He was not fazed one little bit when I presented him with his own letter, with that he then just offered this excuse:

"Sometimes I have a lot of letters placed in front of me, I sign them, and pass them back to my secretary, "he went on to say.

Is it any wonder the civil service is viewed in such a derogatory manner by outsiders?

I made the point that I had made the decision to settle in Dartmouth, based on his offer of a position. He went on to say:

"I will place your name on the list for when a position does arise," that was the only solace I received from him.

I then began the process of trying to obtain a position elsewhere. Iris was not in the job market, as taking care of her mother was full-time in itself. Things appeared to be taking a turn for the better when I got a placing with the Canadian National Railway, in their telegram department. Reporting to work one evening after about two weeks, I was greeted by the supervisor who asked me if I knew about "bumping." The term was completely foreign to me, until he explained:

CHAPTER 42

Down at the Dockyard

My first day as a new civilian was upon me. My previous short stint with Cummins diesel was just a passing chapter in my life, and it was best forgotten. I left home with my lunch bucket, a new experience in itself, I received my morning kiss as I left, she wished me good luck, and said:

"I know you are back in your environment, I can feel, and see, the difference in your attitude of life."

My future was on my mind over the fifteen-mile drive to the dockyards. I knew it was going to be difficult for me to enter a communication centre, smaller than some in which I had previously been in charge of, and to know I would again be sitting on the bottom of the totem pole. That is life, it was truly a new beginning.

Any doubts on my ability to accept that position, was soon put to the rest. I reported to the new office, and my new boss, immediately informed me, she new my experience was much more than what a CM1 was required to know:

"I would appreciate it if you realise, from the start, your position in the chain of command, and act accordingly." She continued.

The minute she introduced me to my fellow workers I knew where she had been coming from, indeed, I was at the lowest point in my career. I found myself duplicating messages on a Gestetner machine, long before the time of Xerox, cranking a handle endlessly for hours on end. The other CM1 on my shift, was a real character, Shirley by name, she became my supervisor, in her eyes at least.

Returning home that night, Iris naturally asked me how I had made out, I laughed, and then filled her in on my exalted position. Life had been kind to me, I had been given opportunities, which I had seized upon, and always made the most of them, this was another of those times.

Within three months of commencing work in the dockyard message centre, natural attrition had made vacancies in all of the communication categories.

Competitions were to be held for the CM 1 to CM 7 slots, I undertook each test separately. I must be careful here that I do not appear to have a large ego, however, facts are facts, and I passed all of these with no problems at all.

I took advantage of these opportunities, and immediately assumed the vacant position as a CM3 for two weeks, before moving up to become the shift supervisor. Poor Shirley, who had achieved such a powerful position bossing me around for a while, was now my chief Gestetner operator.

My home life had taken a dramatic change with the advent of my mother-in- law. She was a really good person, and our relationship was always good, with one exception, this came much later when she was beginning to show signs of dementia. On one of the visits from my brother-in-law, she told him that I had hit her, which of course was in her imagination.

I missed the intimacies of our living together, the pat, the squeeze, on my partners derriere, when helping with the dishes, the stolen kiss, the spontaneous linking of mind and body that had become second nature to us.

I developed a great interest in gardening, so it gave me great pleasure, when folks from the city, would stop on their way to the beach, and compliment me on my "English Garden," as some of them referred it to.

Another indulgence that gave me great pleasure, was to write in the local magazine, from which two ladies were trying to glean a living from. It started as everything usually did for me, by accident.

This led to a regular subscription by me, under the nom de plume of "Pollution Pete." When this turned out to be quite controversial, but very popular with the locals, it was not one of Iris's favourites.

There were those who would have hung me from the nearest tree, if my identity and ever become known.

One day I was babysitting with her mother, when Iris came back from a meeting grinning from ear to ear:

"What do you think? I am now the branch Secretary," she said.

"You do not know the first thing about being a secretary," I replied:

"No but you do" she quickly retorted.

It turned out she was right, she took the notes, I put them on paper, what a relationship, boy did she know the right buttons to push.

That is not quite true, as I was dealing with the Navy now which basically operates under the same communication rules as the Army and Air Force. One of the exceptions is the submarine of which I had no prior knowledge. On my test a question posed to me was:

"You are the supervisor and you have a high precedence message for a submarine, how do you get it to them?"

Using my army knowledge, where you get it to the nearest unit I replied:

"You get it to the nearest ship."

"What do you do then?" The questioner asked.

I was stumped, he went on to explain to me that in actual fact the nearest ship to the submarine drops three hand grenades to inform the vessel to surface. I was to quickly learn many more idiosyncrasies of submarines and the Navy.

One night while assuming duty on the midnight shift, we received a report of a submarine down. Knowing the importance of this I quickly enabled the protocol for such an occasion. Recognising the danger of this, the adrenaline really charges through your veins. For several hours we were engaged with Search and Rescue, in communicating to search vessels and other personnel engaged in the operation.

From the window of our office we saw the activity as the duty ship steamed up ready for sailing. We witnessed the crew arriving in top speed in readiness to aid their fellow mariners. No need for uniforms, manning the ship does not need such niceties as uniforms in an emergency.

Realizing this is not a pleasant thing, the mere fact of being engaged and contributing, gives you a feeling of accomplishment. Five hours later we were to learn that this was a planned sub down, this information did not take away the exhilaration we all felt. Knowing that, had it actually been the real thing, those men would have received the utmost attention in their peril. For most exercises we are pre-warned, for this one we were not.

With about two more years to go before my retirement, the computer began to make itself felt in the communication field. With that came a decline in the requirements, on the knowledge side of supervising. The job became mundane. The challenge was gradually taken away, I was merely a personnel manipulator. This was not for me.

Coinciding with this, I had to climb four flights of stairs to reach my office, I began noticing that I was having increasing difficulty making it to the top. Tests showed I had developed Angina and an Angiogram was recommended.

At the same time my wife was concerned about the health of her mother, who was now approaching the age of 89. Admitted to the Dartmouth hospital very soon after, she subsequently succumbed to heart failure.

At the roundtable of relatives gathered for the funeral, one brother let it be known that he was considering early retirement, and settling in British Columbia. He suggested to us, that we join him, in a joint venture on the West Coast. The seed was sown, how long it would take before it took root, was still up for discussion.

We had talked about a holiday in Florida during the winter months for several years, but us having Iris's mother living with us, had kept it just to talking. The year following the funeral we were prepared to go. I had sent for brochures, and tentative bookings had been made. At the last moment I decided to postpone it for one more year, probably it was the finances in my money conservative mind.

One typical Nova Scotia winters night, while driving home at midnight, the snow still falling to cover the ice left behind from the initial rain. Little voices kept telling me that if I did not go this year, I would never go.

Waking Iris, I told her of my warning voices:

"No problem," she said "You have had those kinds of thoughts before, we will go." We had a beautiful romantic five weeks at Treasure Island on the West coast of Florida, which we would have missed otherwise. We enjoyed swimming in warm water, followed by aperitifs with the evening buffet at the "Brown Derby" before giving in to the Sting Rays, that invaded the beaches for our last week. A truly wonderful holiday.

Back home we were talking moves, again, it was not really my idea, as we had this place paid and accounted for. We had built completely over the original structure, it was, to all intents and purposes a house. With a one and a half acre of land, added to this an uninterrupted view to the mighty Atlantic on three sides. However, it was cold, snowy, with lots of freezing rain and the short summer. What should we do?

CHAPTER 43

Huge Decision

The weeks following our trip south were very hard on Iris, the thoughts of losing her mother, being uppermost in her mind. I knew that she, like all grieving humans, was experiencing the greatest of grief questions that people get:

"What more could I have done?" There was nothing, for twelve years, she had given her all.

My wife's dedication of love and care for her mother was immeasurable. I had witnessed the anguish of her taking her mother a cup of tea in the morning, then a few minutes later being asked:

"Who was that nice young lady who bought me my tea this morning?"

The endless waiting hand and foot on her mother's frivolous requests, and the timeless demands made on her patience. She loved her mother deeply, and she gave from her heart.

We had the task of settling the small estate in England, Iris was again displaying her selflessness, by dividing it equally four ways, although two of the siblings had contributed nothing at all in the sustenance of their mother, over the past twelve years. If it were at all possible, I cherished her even more through this difficult time.

As hard as it was for her, I would still come home from work, open the door, and be greeted by the delicious aroma of newly baked bread, rolls, and a house clean and tidy, and more importantly, by her

It was only a matter of time before the B.C. question would be posed again. I knew in her heart she was in need of a change. Despite my arguments, about what we possessed here, which was ours in its entirety, no mortgages, or unpaid bills, we were as secure as life could be.

However, I agreed to pursue a move seriously. Resigning from my job in the dockyard, we placed our property on the market. We had one and a half acres of land, half of it cultivated, with lots and flowers, the remainder was in its natural beauty, stretching down to the salt water. An uninterrupted view, with no possibility of it ever being interfered with." Prime property Eh?"

We sold all of this for $49,000 (unbelievable,) as money makers, we left a lot to be desired. For us the move west was soon the wish of my partner, I would go along with it. Her happiness had always been my primary motivation, so why change now?

We purchased a used RV, and as usual for us, we made an extremely bad choice. We had priced a new trailer, which would have made a large dent in our finances, however, had we purchased it, we would have saved ourselves many dollars over the next four thousand miles.

We left our home for a rendezvous with Iris's brother in Toronto. In the meantime, he had placed his house on the market. By the time we had reached Gananoque, we had endured furnace trouble, in addition to that, we had to put a new set of new tires on the trailer, and the door lock and broken.

Anyone reading this epistle must think we had empty spaces in our heads, where our brains should have been. Maybe you are right, through all of this we were still together. We stayed in Toronto for are few days discussing our future journey out West

At last the real trek started, so by using my military background, our route was planned to the minutest detail. It was early October, so we realized we would be just ahead of the snow and winter conditions.

Enjoying stopovers would not be of prime importance. Our mileage would depend on the accommodation at the end of the day, as many of the campsites would be closed. The North American Camp Atlas, was an asset with my planning out our overnight stops.

I had decided the Canadian route was too precarious, weather wise. So, we headed to Detroit, where we entered the U. S. A. and then proceeded south until reaching Interstate eighty. We followed this over to Salt Lake City, where we had planned to stay two or three days for a break.

We were covering, on average at that time, two hundred and fifty miles a day, give or take a mile. After driving several days through Nebraska and Wyoming we entered what appeared to us as the "Garden of Eden" in Utah. The trans-formation from the prairies, where the sight of hundreds of Elk, many of whom, were unfortunately strewn on the side of the interstate.

The last hundred miles out of Wyoming seemed to be a gradual rise, until we arrived at the Utah border, where we were then transcended into a beautiful lush valley, with trees and shrubs and habitation, unbelievable beauty after the flat and uninteresting countryside that we had just experienced.

We proceeded through Salt Lake City, with the intention of reaching our predestined camp site in Ogden. We had planned to take a forty-eight hour stop over there, enabling us to visit the world famed Mormon Tabernacle in SLC.

We arrived in Ogden at noon, the sun was so hot, I had to remove my shirt, as we lunched at the picnic table. We were surrounded by mountains, and were impressed with our good fortune, to have all of this at our disposal.

We could not get over the temperature, the next morning, on looking out of the trailer window, we could not believe our eyes. We were surrounded by three inches of the deadly white stuff.

As the morning progressed, the sun regained its control, and the snow was, completely gone before lunchtime. This gave us the opportunity to travel back a few miles to the city, as we had previously planned to do. If any reader has not seen the tabernacle, and is within one hundred miles of it at any time, do your self a big favour and visit. Words cannot describe the splendour!

Built completely by hand more than one hundred years ago, it is amazing. The organ pipes, golden in colour, and massive in size, were all built by hand of wood. How we wished we could have heard the organ playing, along with the singing of the choir.

The acoustics are absolutely fantastic, the guide stood on the rostrum, we stood at the back of the temple, we heard him drop a small object, the sound was amazing. We were so impressed. Although we were given a guided tour, no claim was made on us for money, or religious pressures placed upon us. This was just one more pleasant memory.

The next day we continued our journey North on highway eighty-four. Over the next few days, we travelled through Idaho into Oregon, along the Columbia River highway to Portland, continuing north up the Olympic Peninsula to Port Angeles.

We paused in Washington state to install two more new tires. From there we crossed the Juan de Fuca straits', to Victoria, and our first initial impression of British Columbia. Our first stop in B.C. was in Victoria, when we arrived, we knew no one, where or where would we locate.?

CHAPTER 44

Reconnaissance

We were not dismayed at being in a strange place with no friends to greet us. This had become the norm for us in our nomadic lifestyle. We left the next morning to investigate the area around Mill Bay. David and Gloria, my wife's brother 's and sister in law were not departing Toronto until they had sold their home.

We had been charged with the proposition of scouting out some properties suitable for multiple living. On a recent visit to the island, they had seen several acreages advertised, that filled this requirement, two houses on one site. This turned out eventually, to be only a pipe dream.

I was now unable to walk much further than a few hundred yards, before developing chest pains, and shortness of breath. The medication I had been prescribed, was acting more like a depressant every day.

Our first contact in Mill Bay was the medical centre, to enlist the services of a Doctor, as recommended by my physician back in Nova Scotia. Arrangements were made for me to see a specialist, with orders from the local medic, to take things carefully. Not an auspicious start for a pioneer from the east!

We parked our recreation vehicle in Mill Bay, and checked out the neighbourhood, and were pleased with what we saw. Coming from the east, we found the prices did seem much higher, food and accommodation for instance. We were certainly not going to get much for $49,000 out here. (Maybe an outhouse.)

There were no properties listed that filled our requirements, so we widened our search as far as Parksville. The time came for my appointment, followed by another Angiogram, which showed a blocked artery, and another, in very poor shape. The specialist did not consider it serious enough for surgery, as he just changed my medication, with the recommendation that I try to walk as much as possible. (Several years later I had a six bypass operation)

It was not long after before David and his wife arrived on the island. The search for a place to call home began with sincerity. The first property we looked over, consisted of five and half acres, a miniature "Buchard Gardens." fruit trees of every imaginable variety, Rhododendrons by the dozen, lawns, and a kitchen garden, large enough to feed a regiment.

I looked down from the patio filled with fear, it seemed that I was the only one who could visualize the amount of work involved to keep this estate just tidy. I was just a voice in the wilderness, it made no difference what my views were.

The outcome was, this was the only property they looked at, and they were prepared to sign right away. There was no mother in law suite, the compromise to that was a two-car garaged, with an unfinished area above, that could be converted into a one-bedroom, kitchen, living room and bath room.

This consumed most of our financial return from the N.S. property. It was tastefully decorated, and furnished, indeed it was a modern and comfortable living area.

We were happy at first, my health improved a little, and I was able to partake in some of the chores, eventually, the kitchen garden became my domain. Iris settled into her baking activities, and life between us was as it had always been.

In the late summer of our first year on the island, we went to England for five weeks, visiting an aunt of my wife, who had remained very close to her, she assisted us with our fare, putting it, in her words that she:

"Would rather give it to Iris and see her now, than leave it in her will, after she had passed away." Very logical of her.

We enjoyed a lovely two week stay with her in West Sussex, a beautiful part of rural Britain. Visits to my wife's sister in Norfolk followed, with some time with my brother in St. Helens, this completed our itinerary. While visiting my brother, we spent some time in the Lake District, a charming area of quietness and beauty.

Following our return, there was a drastic change in my relationship with David's wife, it is of no importance, as to who was to blame, the fact is that it never should have happened. Communications between us deteriorated to a low ebb. Iris was in the middle of the unpleasantness, trying to act as a negotiator. They tried their hardest to come between us, recommending that she kick me out.

Family disputes are usually about nothing of importance; however, they can get very vicious. Nasty words were exchanged, and bridges were broken, that would take a long time to mend, it all culminated with us leaving at very short notice.

We were entering the lowest point of our life together, here we were, approaching our fortieth anniversary, facing a return to a one room apartment, that is not much of an accomplishment for all those years we had been together. It would have been easy for me, to have remonstrated, by saying:

"We had it all, why did you want to leave the good life behind, for this?"

No, this was the time to face the problem together, our small money balance left us in a precarious position. We could not purchase a house; our only alternative was renting. We were short on time to find accommodation, so, we scrutinized the local newspaper, amazed at the very few opportunities we had at our disposal.

At first, we listed vacancies by what we could afford, this opened us up to some awful places. A few of them were so run down, only a bulldozer could improve their appearance.

Poor Iris was in a fit of despair. Our future looked extremely bad, not once did she say she regretted coming to B C or, sticking the blame on me for our limited resources, we would have to tighten our belts and wait out the remaining year, until our Old Age Pension kicked in.

Only one last place was left on our list, appeared that we could afford by scrimping on our limited resources.

Making an appointment with the leaser, we entered what seemed like a palace, compared to what we had seen in the same price range. A double wide mobile, in pretty good condition. Obviously, with the advent of our furniture and affects, we could make it a comfortable home.

The leaser of the property had very strict requirements. We wondered if she would accept that we had no references? we had both entertained the same thoughts. At that moment in time we did not know, that this would turn out to be a five-year relationship, with a wonderful old lady.

She had a small home on the same piece of land which belonged to the mother our future landlord. We were escorted over to meet her, as she was to have the final say, on whether we would be suitable tenants. She greeted us by saying:

"Would you like a cup of tea, ducks," Of course we acquiesced.

"You will have to take me as I am," she went on.

Her modest home was tastefully decorated with nice furniture, dating back a few years, it was almost antique in fact, our hostess was ninety-two years young, as she put it. Her, and my wife, took to each other like two peas in a pod.

"When do you want to move in? she asked.

I am certain that the sighs of relief Iris and I let out, must have sounded like the deflation of a tire on a semi truck:

"Today if possible," we obviously were not expecting too much luck in compliance:

"That is fine," our lovely hostess countered.

Why do we all despair so much in life, there is always sunshine around the next corner? We used our trailer as a moving van, and within the day we had set up in our new home, counting our blessings.

CHAPTER 45

Near Death Experience

The gradual restoration of happiness in the life of Iris was a reward in itself, I had never seen her so dejected and worried before. Her true goodness and positive outlook on life had been given a body blow. In Gram, as we affectionately called her, our beloved landlady, whose personification reminded her so much of her own mother. She and Gram developed a bond that was special.

We took over the job of looking after her, shopping and caring etc. She had helped twice a week with the inside maintenance of the home otherwise, she was self supporting.

We spent hours listening to her reminisce, of how her father had pioneered, and lived on his own in northern Saskatchewan, before sending for her mother and his siblings to join him. She told how they were booked on the ill-fated "Titanic," Fate had entered her life at that time, as the steamship company had offered her mother, an earlier sailing, at a cheaper rate. The hardships and privations she encountered at the age of fourteen on the prairies. She had a story to tell, I would have loved the opportunity to write it.

The first year we were in the double wide my brother and his wife came over from England to help us celebrate our fortieth wedding anniversary. When we were courting, I was unable to buy Iris an engagement ring, it was hard enough to get a wedding band after the war. So, I surprised her by presenting her with a Ruby ring surrounded by small diamonds.

It took her completely by surprise, and except for later visits to the hospital she never left it off after that. We managed to give our visitors an enjoyable holiday. I know they still think of in with great joy.

We followed this up with another visit to England ourselves. The aunt, who was so close to my wife, felt she might only have this visit from us, her premonition came to pass. We stayed with her for the first weeks of our visit. Unfortunately, we were unable to take her out in the car, and her insistence we hired a car to drive around Britain, to the various places we were stationed at during the war.

When we were both serving in the forces, Iris was always stationed in the Northeast, whereas my postings, had been in the Southwest. Neither of us was familiar with each other's area, so we planned this trip around England, as a journey of nostalgia.

This turned out to be a great idea, we relived those years, and were able to explain the highs and lows of each of those postings, to each other, it was much more rewarding than we had first imagined.

On our return to Canada we began one of the happiest associations of our entire married life. We took our cat to the vet's office one day, and read a poster on the wall for Square Dance lessons. My better half informed me that she had always wanted to do that:

"Let us go and see what it is like," she said.

I was reticent to say the last.

When we entered the hall in Duncan, there were not too many folks present, one person we did notice, he was up on the small stage, dressed like Roy Rogers. Several of the ladies were in their square-dancing dresses, Iris was quick to let me know she thought that the ladies' outfits were lovely.

"Mr. Rogers" got us on the floor in circles of eight, and a he soon had us moving to the left, and introduced us to our first, and certainly not the last, "Left Allemande"

We stopped for a moment, while his wife told us the importance of deodorant, Roy Rogers turned out to be our club caller, and he, and his wife, became two of our best friends ever.

I have never known my wife to instantly enjoy herself as she did here, she radiated it every time we attended a dance. I was so happy to see her in her dresses, with the swinging crinolines, as I have said previously, she never dressed to show off, it just made her feel good.

We made many friends in a very short time, one couple took us under their wing at the beginner's classes. He escorted Iris, while his wife Donna, took me in tow, they also are great friends to this day.

Our elation was short-lived however, as one night with no prior warning, she woke me at two am, she was out of bed, lying on the floor, her breathing sounded awful, just like the death rattles, that I had been told about in my youth.

She was in a dreadful mess; she had not wanted to wake me up. I immediately dialled 911 for an ambulance, and tried to make her comfortable.

Our elation was short lived however. One night with no prior warning, Irish woke me at 2 AM breathing sounded awful, just like the death rattles, that I had been told about in my youth. The blade was in a dreadful mess, she had not wanted to wake me.

I immediately dialled 911 for an ambulance and tried to make her as comfortable as I could. There was little communication between us, as she was almost in a coma, I was so scared. The medics eventually arrived and took her in the ambulance to Duncan

Hospital. They told me not to follow them, as it was snowing really hard, and the roads were treacherous, but nothing would stop me from accompanying her.

She was admitted immediately to the ICU, and the prognosis was Sepsis. I waited in the quiet room, while they got settled. The doctor eventually came and informed me, that they did not know quite what was happening, but she was in a serious condition. He said:

"We have given her strong medication, and if she makes it to the morning, we have a chance," he went on to say "You can see her for a few minutes, but she will not know you."

I could tell she was near death, her face was so white, her breathing still making that awful noise. I drove home convinced in my own mind; I was going to lose her.

For over a week she laboured between life and death, not fully in a coma, but incoherent and hallucinating. On the days leading up to her illness, she had been engaged in Christmas preparation, baking, cakes and mince pies etc. On one of my visits she told me to bring the nurses some nice mince tarts, the next time I visited the hospital.

I did this, and she greeted me by saying:

"Why don't you go home, you old fuddy duddy."

The tone in her voice was venomous, the nurse noticed, and she took my hand saying:

"She does not mean it; she is not understanding what she is saying."

None the less, it hurt all the same.

During the second week she showed signs of improvement, the doctors and nurses were pleased, nowhere near so much as me. At the end of the third week she was discharged, but she was never the same after that.

We continued our dancing, but Iris had to start sitting out

more dances, her energy level had been so reduced. I found myself doing more jobs around the house, preparing a few more meals than previously. This was a small price to pay for having her with me. I was to have ten more years, although there was no way of knowing it then.

CHAPTER 46

Feline Fancier

As I prepared myself for writing this chapter in our lives, I realised that there was another side to my Iris, that I had passed over. It was indeed, a large part of our happiness together, and it needs some exposure. Along with all the other loving attributes I have written about her, her love of all animals was yet another demonstration of why she will get her just reward in heaven.

She always had seed for the birds, sugar water for the hummingbirds, and scraps for the cat strangers that came around the door. However, her greatest love was reserved for cats.

Iris related a story that may have been the seed for this passion for felines. When she was of kindergarten age, her family had a cat that was not the best house trained animal of all time. He had a nasty habit of raising his tail, to spray his territory, whenever, and where ever, the need came over him.

One day he did it over the basket of freshly washed linen. Iris's mother was not too impressed with that, so, she made the decision to tell her husband that the poor animal must go. Fearful of the damage it might do to her daughter they told her that it had drowned, as they lived by the sea, this excuse was logical, but highly doubtful. On learning of the demise of her dear "Puss" she cried her heart out and said:"My poor Puss was dwounded. (Little girl talk.)

We picked up our first stray when staying with the Colonel and his alcoholic wife. We named it Fluffy for obvious reasons. He became a much-travelled cat, crossing the Atlantic on three occasions.

His first venture at this, was accompanying us when we immigrated to Canada. He returned again when Iris went back to England, while I was in Egypt. Due to Great Britain's archaic rules the cat had to spend six months in quarantine. As his kennel was more than 100 miles from where Iris was staying, he did not receive many visits.

He was never the same after that confinement, returning with us to spend his last days in Edmonton.

He was the only cat we had that travelled well in an automobile. On one occasion, sitting on the back of the passenger seat, with his tail up against his mistresses' neck, as we were not as well clued up in those days, and did not have the common sense to have a litter box with us. One day, after driving many hours, he christened Iris with a stream of hot water. All down her back.

Needless to say, the next motel became our haven, and a kitty litter box was our first priority. Fluffy passed away while I was in Kingston on a course, so I was unable to console her in the loss. He had been our companion for 15 years.

We moved to Wainwright in Alberta shortly after that. One day a stray cat came meowing at the door, Iris, good Samaritan as she always was, took it in, fed it, fell in love, and gave it a home. He was given the name of Smoky, as his coat resembled that colour.

We did not have him very long, he died under anaesthetic while being neutered. Iris was very upset, as she felt the kitten had no say in his demise, and had not been sick.

The next edition was Tinker, who had two important stories in his life. We had moved to Ottawa by then, where we lived in a ground floor apartment. Iris left the window slightly open for the cat's convenience.

One morning as she was preparing to go to work, we got a phone call informing us that our cat had been run over. I obtained a spade, proceeded to the scene of the accident, gathered him gently in my arms and carried him to the spot that I would lay him to rest.

A few minutes after I had completed this extremely unpleasant task, Tinker came through the window to rub around our legs. Later that day, a lady came to the door, asking if we had buried a cat, and where?

I accompanied her to the spot and exhumed the unfortunate animal for the distressed owner. The cat was so much like Tinker it is understandable why I could have made such a mistake.

We kept him throughout our stay in the capital city, then he came with us to Truro, Nova Scotia, where he enjoyed the run of a large field next to our property. He earned his keep, by killing dozens of mice. He had a six months vacation in Ontario with us, while I was on an upgrading course in Kingston, and was a constant companion for my wife.

On our return to Truro, we purchased our first mobile home and moved to what at first seemed to be an equally ideal spot. We were wrong with that assumption.

One morning at 5 a.m. he woke us up to go out. A few minutes later we heard yelping dogs running by our mobile home. Later, when Tinker had not returned, we searched and found him 6 feet from a hydro pole, that he obviously had tried to escape to. His neck had been broken by the dogs.

Shortly after we left Truro for Kingston, we adopted another waif. This one we named Toby, and he turned out to be a real character. We think he must have been part Lynx, as he had huge tufts of hair growing from the tips of his ears, which made him look very different to a normal cat.

He couldn't be called a loving animal either, as with all her love given to him by my wife she could not really get to this one. Still, there was no way she would part with him, so off to Germany we went.

We boarded him on Air Canada in Ottawa, bound for Dusseldorf in Germany, as the Military would not allow animals on their aircraft. On our arrival, he was supposed to be at the airport, ready to be picked up. Alas on arriving, there was no Toby, the attendant made several calls throughout the airline's facilities, where they finally located the cat, he was in Berlin, so the next day he was reunited with a very loving "mother!" He had been where we were not allowed to go, behind the Iron Curtain.

This cat met a very sad end, as returning from a shopping trip we called out for him, he ran to us, and jumped on a chair under a table. We found him minutes later straddled across his litter box, with his legs splayed out behind him. Iris gently picked him up, and we rushed to the veterinarian in the nearby town

An x-ray discovered he had broken his back, so we had no option but to put him to rest. Iris was devastated, I had seen her under just about every situation I could think of, in our life together, but this was so hurtful.

She was always so loving and kind to all of her animals, forever trying to spread goodness around. I could never understand why she had to suffer with every animal she loved.

Germany was not a cat loving country, especially in the northern part where we now lived. It looked as if we had to wait until our return to Canada before we could get another feline companion.

Iris felt that part of her life was missing, without a cat in the house. We heard of a pet shop in Dusseldorf advertising a Siamese kitten for sale. We immediately jumped in the car to locate the premises, only to find it was a dead end, as they had no cat.

He did give us an address in another small town, where possibly we could obtain one. Imagine the joy we had, when we saw this poor little creature, hunched up in the corner of the cage, looking as if death would be better than where it found itself.

She was in terrible shape, mites in its ears, fur missing, and it looked underfed. It was a candidate for adoption as soon as Iris saw it. As poorly as it looked, it had a pedigree with a European champion on one side. Obviously, the breeding had not stood it in a good stead. It had a special breeders name "Bene Von De Kaiser Falze" (Bee from the Emperor's Castle) we took her home with us.

What a treat she turned out to be, we had never previously wanted a Siamese cat, we soon discovered what a difference they are, to the ordinary house cats. We kept Tina (for that was her name) for 10 years, before she succumbed with diabetes.

By this time, we were back in Nova Scotia, where we picked up another Siamese, this one we christened Mia. Two years following that, we adopted another Siamese, this one became Midget, we had to change her name to Midge, as she grew up to be no midget.

They were the talk with everyone who visited. They were always together, paws wrapped around each other, Mia died at 17, two years later Midget passed at the age of 15. She was the only one cremated, we kept her ashes, and I decided to place them in the coffin, to be buried with Iris.

We did not know it at that time, but my wife had only a few more months to live. We had gone about five weeks, when we decided that we would not have have another, as it would not be fair on the animal.

One evening my wife said to me:

"I think we should get another cat, if anything happened to one of us it would be company for the other." Words of wisdom, or was it yet another case of fate? We went to the local pet shop and picked up Muffin, a Himalayan.

The cat bonded to me right away, the first one to ever do that, so it seems much like fate, as a few weeks later my Iris was gone, she must have had a premonition. Muffin became a real companion to me.

I cannot see my screen at the moment for tears, my composure has broken down, I feel she was thinking of me and my future happiness.

CHAPTER 47

Still Time to Play

Having Gram in our lives added a whole new dimension to our daily living.

Iris showed so much improvement in her daily life, all brought on by her contacts with that wonderful old lady. It would appear that it should have been the other way around, but Gram was so wise, she imparted a new outlook on life for my wife.

Her encouragement got my love and I, to start walking regularly. She also accompanied us with these daily endeavors. Iris's general health improved to a point where she began baking again, she was also able to do more around the house, and became more active in her favourite pastime, Square dancing.

The old lady's help was not just confined to Iris, on one occasion I remarked to her, that I had a fear of Alzheimer's disease, Gram responded by commenting:

"I have seen your aptitude for writing, you should get yourself a computer."

On purchasing one, I commenced writing, when ever I could, I undertook the Historian position with our dance club, and became the club secretary.

She constantly advised us that we should write to Iris's brother for some recompense, from our contribution to the property. Iris was adamantly opposed to this. She had no desire to extend this separation, but she was ever hoping for a phone call of reconciliation, and apology.

For my part, I considered her feelings, and waited until she decided whether or not to proceed with a letter. In due course this recourse was undertaken, and an agreeable settlement was accomplished, without further stretching the relationship.

The improvement in my wife's health, justified us to undertake a holiday in the USA, our first since settling on the island. We decided to spend the Christmas break in Los Angeles, flying with Delta Airlines, where we stayed at the Howard Johnson In in Anaheim.

This allowed us to participate on excursions without exposing Iris to too much exertion. We spent two days in the Disney empire, which, in our eyes, did not compare with its partner in Orlando, Florida, which had a newer and additional attraction called "Epcot."

This additional area, contains the exhibitions of various countries, where you can indulge in their cuisines and customs etc. We really enjoyed a day at Universal Studios, which included a ride on the spectacular Earthquake, and the Parting of the sea, from the two movies.

We had two bus trips, one to San Diego, where we visited Sea World, where we both had nauseous attacks, following a seafood meal. Fortunately, one trip to the toilet was sufficient to clear up the problem, allowing us to enjoy the rest of the trip.

The other excursion we undertook, was to Tijuana, Mexico. This Mexican town reminded me of my days in the Gaza Strip, the bargaining, and the unpleasant odours. We did enjoy a couple of margaritas however.

It was good for me to see Iris enjoying herself once again, to be more like she had been prior to her illness. We had a memorable time and was sorry when the week was over.

We had lived in the double wide mobile for close to five years, and we started expressing fears that when Gram passed away, as, unbelievably she was now ninety-seven. At that time we thought her son and daughter in all possibility would want to put the property up for sale, we would then probably face the position of being evicted.

I had noticed for some time, that Iris had been paying more attention to the Real Estate sections of the local newspaper. One day she drew my attention to a mobile home situated on its own, on lot in Ladysmith, suggesting that we go and take a look.

This turned out to be a dump, not acceptable at any cost. The real estate person told us of another trailer on the subdivision, which we subsequently inspected, and deposited a down payment. We accepted the fact that we would be moving yet again. When would it ever stop?

The next day a friend of whom we had notified of our purchase, and who was in the building business, telephoned us, and said:

"I hope you do not mind, but I took a look at that property, and you should do everything in your power to get out of it, it is a real bad investment."

Apparently, he had gotten underneath, something we had not thought of doing, and he discovered structural deterioration, so in a panic, we contacted the real estate agent, to tell him what we had just found out, requesting the possibility that he might have another unit we could exchange for it.

At the same time, we had noticed a small house in the same location, and inquired if it was on his list, if so, could we view it.? Good fortune awaits those that have patience, the house was quite a bit more expensive, only six months old, and naturally, it was in perfect condition.

For the first time in our lives, we threw caution to the wind, and went for it. We signed on the bottom line, and we were to have almost eight, very happy years living there.

It was one of the most difficult times of our lives when we informed our landlady of our pending departure. She was so very disappointed.

We assured her we would get down to visit her, every opportunity we could, indeed on her next birthday, we arranged with some of our friends, to give her a potluck lunch.

We surprised her on the day, with a visit, we had a birthday cake and a bottle of wine. She also had friends visiting her from Saskatchewan. They joined in with us in celebrating her ninety eighth birthday. She went to bed that night, and passed away in her sleep. It was the peaceful ending that she had, and was only what she deserved.

There was no memorial service or obituary. Iris was most disturbed, that no one in her family, had found it appropriate, to put an obituary in print, for this great lady, who had lived such a long and eventful life.

That, after all, was my wife, the difference in outlook and caring for others that I had been fortunate enough to share.

CHAPTER 48

The Big 50

The next period of our lives would be full of happy times with memorable events, how I wish those years could have been extended to take in the present. I would not now be engaged in writing the final chapters of our wonderful life together.

It was fitting that there were so many good times, Iris was thrilled with our latest home, insisting we make some improvements, such as installing an asphalt driveway, and a concrete path way to the front door, and build a wooden fence.

I was satisfied with the status quo, but again my Iris always had more foresight than I. It was a small residence as they go today, but it was ours, she was proud of It, as I was always proud of her.

There were two things in our married life that had given me personal hurts. Number one, I always wanted to redo our vows. When I asked, Iris she never made any comment, it was as if she had not heard me. The second, was my telling her how much she had always meant to me,

"I would do it all over again, would you? I frequently asked her:

"I don't know," she always replied.

This could have fallen into the same category, as her ongoing difficulty in expressing her love for me, in words. Her nonchalance over those two questions, often made me feel deeply hurt, I could not understand why.

We were content to enjoy the beauties of the island, rarely leaving to visit the mainland. We were flattered when John, our square dance caller, and his wife, asked us to join them for three weeks at Pia Pica close to San Diego. Iris and Carol spent their time together at the pool, while we men went down to the beach in San Diego, looking for hidden treasure.

John had bought one of those metal detectors to find his fortune. He waved his magic wand over the sand, while I did the digging, we found no gold rings, just a few quarters and nickels, and an awful lot of those tags off the top of aluminum cans. It would take a long time for him to recoup his outlay, but it was fun.

We spent one day in Yuma, Arizona, where we were fortunate enough to hit the day, they had a street market. The girls found a stall selling Square dance dresses, so this enabled my dear wife to add yet more dresses to her wardrobe.

John and I shared the driving chores, and it fell on me to navigate Los Angeles in both directions. That was an experience to be remembered. I had witnessed it many times on television, however, it has to be done personally to fully comprehend the ordeal of it.

To glance in the rear-view mirror and see twelve lanes of desperate motorists bearing down on you, makes the "Charge of the light brigade" seem like a class B movie.

For some time, I had been mentally planning a surprise party for my lady, for our fiftieth anniversary. I was going to have a catered meal in the hall, that our club used, followed by a square dance.

My first requirement of course, was to find a caller, as you cannot square dance without one. Naturally I contacted my friend John, to engage his services. He promptly told me:

"It will be an honour, I will do it gladly, you do not have to engage me, I will do it for free."

This started a snowball effect, as Carol, his wife, contacted some of our closest friends, who took the project completely out of my hands.

It was a proud night for us. We were deeply touched. Iris had bought a three-piece navy-blue suit, with white piping, she looked just wonderful. I have the whole evening on video, and watched her expressions, ranging from embarrassment, to near tears, as the evening expanded. Did she ever have any thoughts of the past?

Of course, she had got me new clothes for the occasion. What was supposed to be a big secret, soon became common knowledge to everyone. Carol had made us a beautiful cake, decorated with an ornament of a couple on top. We were sitting at the head table, with linen tablecloths, and the best of cutlery.

Two golden coloured candles were lit, and champagne poured, just for us. My friend Gordon, an ex-military buddy of thirty-five years, roasted us. I gathered up the courage, and gave a prepared speech, outlining our life together.

I simply cannot do justice to the evening, sixty-seven of our friends had felt they wanted to join us, on this auspicious occasion. There were more who would have attended, had it not been a long weekend in the summer, when a lot of folks are vacationing.

Many times, following that evening, we have reiterated, how glad we were, that we had partaken in those dancing lessons, to meet these wonderful outgoing folks, who had contributed so much, in celebrating our fifty years together.

We were so on high at that time. It has been hard to imagine that our partnership, was so close to ending.

CHAPTER 49

Roller Coaster Ride

On February twenty fifth, I felt under the weather, the next day I fitfully dozed on and off all day, covered by a blanket, in my favourite Lazy Boy chair. We both thought I had a bout of the flu. Iris seemed to be hyper active all day, she completed two washes, ironed, baked muffins, and hoovered. She appeared to be consumed with the idea of getting everything, and everywhere, cleaned up.

My efforts to slow her down, were met with indifference, and annoyance. I have said many times, that I was unable to tell her to do anything, even for her own good, this was just another occasion.

She found time to see to my needs, she had great faith in that old remedy of Chicken stew. I could smell its aroma permeating from the kitchen. Her anxiety however was of concern to me.

The next day on waking, she informed me that she did not feel too good, and maybe had contacted the flu, that I had been down with. I arose and made a pot of tea, which was my first normal function of every day.

Her lethargy was obvious, so I suggested she stay in bed, and I told her I would prepare her breakfast, notice, I only suggested. She told me that all she wanted was toast, I did manage to get her to stay in bed long enough for her to eat it.

She then got up, had her ablutions, and put on her housecoat, before settling on the settee. My long association with her, allowed me to know when she was not well. I nursed her throughout the day, pleading with her to go to the emergency, with only negative results.

Her condition did not appear to be really severe, but she was showing many of the symptoms she had displayed with the Sepsis. She retired early, and went to sleep right away. I had no need to be overly worried.

I was awakened by hearing her calling my name in a very weak voice, I reached across the bed, to find her spot vacant. Jumping out, I quickly found her sprawled on the bedroom floor, obviously in a very serious condition. It was only 2 am.

Realizing it was serious, I dialled 911 for an ambulance, I returned to make her more comfortable. I placed a pillow under her head and cleaned up some of the mess surrounding her. The ambulance attendants made a quick evaluation and took her to the Chemainus Hospital. The local doctor diagnosed her, as suffering from the flu, and admitted her.

The next day I visited her again in the hospital, and there did not appear to be any worsening of her condition. She was able to converse, she did, however, have a trace of the rattle, so predominant as she had displayed ten years previously. I visited her throughout the day, then I left with no undue concern.

In the late evening of February twenty fifth, (that night) the roller coaster for both of us began in earnest. I was awakened by a ringing of the telephone, to be told by the nurse in Chemainus hospital, that Iris had been rushed to the Duncan Hospital, and was admitted to the ICU.

I dressed quickly and rushed into Duncan. On entering the facility, a nurse directed did me to the quiet area informing me that the doctor would be down as soon as possible, to discuss my wife's condition.

"Your wife appears to have had a massive heart attack, at this moment she is in a coma," he informed me.

"Have you, or your wife, ever discussed "Life Support?

"No" I replied,

"I will place her on it right away," he said,

There was no hesitation on my part to agree to this.

He informed me I that could see her for a few minutes, when they had completed their procedure. I spent two long, sad hours, before the nurse directed me in to see my wife.

I have never seen so many intravenous bags attached to one patient in my life. She lay on her back, her face seemed almost waxen, a huge tube was inserted in her throat, and plastic tubes seeming to be entering her body in every conceivable place

It was heart rendering, I kissed her forehead, the only place I could make contact with, trying to hide my tears from the nursing staff. The doctor asked me to go, as they had more work to do.

I must have driven home on autopilot. I could not remember a single thing of the journey. I went directly to the bedroom, to be greeted by an horrendous mess.

Apparently, she had set out for the bathroom, but overcome by fatigue, she must have laid down on the floor, and lost control of her body functions. She had vomited, normally this would have turned my stomach, I guess love, has a way of neutralizing such emotions, thank goodness we had a carpet cleaner.

The next five days I spent every available minute beside my wife. It was gut wrenching to see her expressionless face, the slight rise and fall of her chest, which was the only visible sign that she was still alive.

The nurses told me to keep talking to her, as the medical profession did not know if patients could, or could not, hear when in a coma. I needed no prodding. I held her hand, touched her cheeks, and frequently kissed her.

My whole life was laying before my eyes, my reason for living, everything I had ever wanted. The future for me look very barren.

Her brother David, had surprised me, by ringing and asking if he could visit her. I asked him to wait until she had recovered, in order for me to ask her if that was her wish. I further informed him, that I personally had no objections of him seeing her. He agreed to this arrangement, and I promised him, that I would keep him informed daily of his sister's progress.

By this time, the doctor had changed his prognosis, and he said she did have a return of Sepsis.

On the sixth day of coma, the doctor informed me they were going to take her to the Nanaimo hospital for a Cat Scan and Brain evaluation, and that she would be away until about one thirty. This gave me the morning off, but it did not alleviate the worry and the concern, in fact it increased.

I was at the hospital long before the estimated time of her return, accompanied by Win, Iris's closest and best friend and her husband Dick. David and Gloria were also there.

The doctor came in and informed us, that the test had shown that Iris had very little brain activity, and that she could be a vegetable, if she did survive. I had to make the hardest decision of my life to take her off Life Support.

I knew at that time, it would not be my wife's wish to become a liability, and although it was an unbearable thought, I decided that it would be for the best.

This action was undertaken at 4 pm, we all stayed for a while, then I was on my own with her. The doctor had told us, it could take from four hours to four days for her to give up on life.

My decision was to spend every minute I could with her. I could not believe my actions over the next twenty-four hours. I was actually asking her to give up, to stop the fight, and join her mother in heaven.

My heart was broken, I knew Iris would want me to let her go. I stayed all night. The nurses were very helpful to me. They implored me to try and get some rest, gave me a pillow and blanket, and took me to the Chesterfield in the quiet room, where they told me they would wake me if anything happened. I tried, but I could not rest, my place was beside my dear one.

At seven in the morning, I drove home for a shower, and some breakfast. If you have ever eaten something with no taste to it, you will know the feeling. I was back beside the bed by nine o'clock and spent the day with her.

Win and her husband visited the Hospital every day, and today was no different. They entered the ward around 4 pm to help me with my vigil. We had no expectations; we just had a common desire to be with her when she met her Lord.

Twenty-four hours, almost to the minute, Iris moved her legs, she was trying to shift her position in bed. Expressions began to replace the deadpan look that we had got used to seeing. Her eyes opened, she tried to smile, and then to talk, the tube in her throat restricted this. She obviously had recognized us.

There was no brain damage, the relief for all of us was a showing by our tears of relief. I ran for the nurse, who told Iris to squeeze, first her right, and then her left hand. The nurse arranged for us to see the doctor right away, he asked us:

"Are you sure she did indeed recognize you?"

"There is no doubt." I answered:

"Okay," he said,

"I will tell the nurse and resume the treatment."

We stayed for a while, then left telling her we would be back the next day. We realized that she was still very sick, but the improvement buoyed all our spirits for the first time in a week.

I informed David right away, I was later to learn that he, and his wife, had visited her the previous evening, and they had mended their bridges. At least some good had emerged from this horrible ordeal. I knew Iris would be at peace with that.

On arriving home, I asked myself:

"What will tomorrow bring?"

CHAPTER 50

The Roller Coaster Continues

I was amazed when I checked into the ICU the next morning, only to find out that they had discharged my wife to the main hospital ward. This was completely beyond my comprehension, to think that, for someone who had been as sick as she was, would be put out on the ward in less than twelve hours.

It was a Saturday, the nursing staff would be on weekend mode, Iris would still need careful supervision. Her room number was 207, a number that will never be erased from my memory. I found her, she was sitting, partly raised, in her bed. She smiled, obviously pleased to see me. Her face was very pale, she looked very weak.

Immediately, on seeing me, she tried to speak, her voice was scratchy from having the tube inserted down her throat, for such a long time. I leaned close, first to kiss her, and tell her I loved her, then ultimately, to understand what she was saying. It was so nice to hear her in such a good spirit, after what she had been through, I could not believe my good fortune

Excusing myself for a few minutes, I hurried down to the nearest florist to purchase the largest bouquet of roses in the store. Blood red, with one pink, a token of my love. I could not wait to return to her side with them, to see her reaction.

It was so rare of me to buy flowers:

"Let me smell them," was her first reaction, "they are beautiful, thank you."

Lunch time came, but she was not on solid food yet, I was not hungry, we just sat down to enjoy each other's company, I felt so happy.

During the afternoon the friends started dropping in, the jungle drums must have been working overtime. The room was soon filled with plants and flowers. The show of love for Iris was overwhelming, forcing me to be just an onlooker.

Her little Asian nurse (who was so caring) was constantly coming in, checking her progress and needs. As evening approached, I leaned over and told her I would not come in that evening, she was tired from visitation, she needed rest. I regret that decision to this day!

Sunday morning, I was in as early as I was allowed, what a joy! She was so much better than the previous day, her voice was stronger. The improvement was easy to see, my visit was a pure pleasure, I could not believe my good fortune, my sweetheart was going to make it. We would be able to enjoy our love together for a while longer.

More visitors dropped in to see her in the afternoon. The comments from Iris were just lovely to hear.

To one friend, who had recently changed her hairstyle, she remarked:

"I do love your hair Beverly, it suits you."

Beverly had brought her a Beamie Baby, like a Siamese cat.

Iris fondled it, displaying her pleasure at receiving such a thoughtful present. Before we left to go home, we placed it on Iris's chest, just to comfort her in some way.

She greeted another visitor by saying:

"What a pretty blouse, and such a lovely colour."

Win, who had been such a good friend, teased her by saying:

"Who brought you those lovely roses," she looked at me with that look of devilment, that we shared between us, that was ours alone.

Her one wish to the nurse all day, was to get her a cup of tea. The Asian nurse, who had been so attentive, came in and told Iris:

"You have your wish, the doctor says you can have your tea, but be careful."

My wife dispatched me in a hurry to the nurses' station to procure it, showing that she was regaining the spirit which only I understood.

She was having difficulty holding, the tea, and then getting it to her mouth, but she waved off my attempt to help her. She looked at her visitors, and smilingly, said:

"He is trying to steal my tea." that was typical of the woman I had known all those years.

I accompanied each of them to the door when they left, and they were so pleased, and amazed, at her progress. At suppertime, I again let it be known to her that I would give up the evening visit to let her rest, why did I do that? I have asked myself so many times since.

Her brother David and Gloria had visited her the previous evening, and did so again in the evening, so she was not alone. Maybe that was better. For the first time in two weeks I went home happy. Would I be happy this time tomorrow night?

CHAPTER 51

Negligence and Incompetency

I could not wait to get in to see my love on Monday, March the eighth, I had been so high the previous day I found it difficult to sleep. The roller coaster for Iris had been much more demanding on her, than on me, however, by the same token, it had made its claim on me.

It was right on 10 am when I entered her room. Our own Dr. was sitting by the bedside chatting to her. I asked her first, if she would like a cup of tea:

"Please, I would love one." she said.

I told the Dr. I would like to have a word with him before he left. He joined me in the kitchen, as I made the tea:

"I am very pleased with Iris" he said "it is a miracle" he went on to say:

"She will need help at home, but I know you will be there to give her that."

What more satisfaction could I receive than his words "I am pleased." I took the tea down to her,

"You do know I love you" I said. You can never imagine my joy when she replied:

"I love you too." (She had not said that, for a long time.)

She had been sitting in a chair for about half an hour before I came in. This was the first time since her admittance to the hospital, that she had been able to sit outside of the bed. Soon after my arrival, she told me she was uncomfortable sitting upright, her bare feet not touching the ground:

"I do not think I am getting enough oxygen." she said.

To my dying, day I will always regret my total ignorance of the importance of oxygen in the medical world. If I had not been so ignorant, the resulting few hours may have been different.

I approached the RN in charge of Iris, informing her that her patient was not comfortable, and expressing to her that she did not think she was getting enough oxygen. Her reply was most rude. It gave me the impression; I was just another visitor trying to make her day harder.

"She has to stay up until lunchtime." she snapped She made no effort to check her patient's physical well-being, or investigate the oxygen request that I had made. Many nurses have told me since then, that the mere mention of the word oxygen, should have set off alarm bells in her head.

Lunch time came, I tried to feed her a little soup and dessert. I noticed she was not so sharp, as when I had arrived. As it was lunch time, with no sign of the nurse, I set out to find her. She was in an adjacent ward:

"I thought you were coming to put my wife to bed at lunchtime," I said:

"I am too busy with another admission, I will get there when I can," again, that tone of annoyance, that someone should challenge her authority.

Eventually she did deign to drop in and put Iris to bed. Our friend Win arrived at the same time. While all through this time, my wife had complained of having cold feet in particular, and feeling cold all over. I noticed that the oxygen meter was on the bed, and it only registered eighty-five on both sides. The nurse re-entered the room, asking us to leave. (It had now been five hours since she had last been in the room.)

Immediately following our departure from the room, a doctor rushed down the hallway, he had five nurses in attendance, one nurse carrying an oxygen bottle, and another pushing a portable x-ray machine.

I knew immediately that my wife was in trouble. A short time later another nurse came to our room to say your wife wants to see you. I doubted that very much, it was obvious as soon as we saw her, that her end was very close.

Within minutes, her breathing became noticeably shallower, I held her hand, I knew I was about to lose her, I did not have time to say goodbye.

My wife was about to join her mother in heaven. At ten that morning, she was talking of coming home, asking how her little cat was, and at four in the afternoon, she had left us.

The hardest part of my grieving has been, what might have been? What if the nurse had done what she had sworn to do when she entered the nursing profession? Just how much did her blatant disregard for her patient contribute to her passing? I will never know.

I have heard that people say strange things at the passing of a loved one. I was no different. I told her sleeping body that I had always loved, and had always been true, and had never stepped out of my marriage bonds.

What a different man left the hospital that afternoon, to the one who had arrived so enthusiastically in the morning. I was too numb to really comprehend what had just happened.

The offending nurse is probably still on the ward, still responsible for attending to those who are in need of her services. I pray with all my heart, she at least learned from this experience, to listen to complaints from other patients, to at least check in with them, on a regular basis.

To be alerted, as any trained nurse would be, that the words "lack of oxygen" suspected, or otherwise, is a major signal of possible distress. I did not know this,

"I do now!"

On February Seventeenth, Iris was on a film laughing, full of life, seated beside me, as I blew out my candles. There was no possible way, that either of us, could vaguely visualize, that she would no longer be with us in such a short time.

CHAPTER 52

Closing of the Ranks

For many months following my loss, I investigated every area I could manage to bring the gross incompetency of this particular nurse out in the open. Not for retribution, or financial gain, on my part, but simply to alert the public at large, of the state of the nursing care in our institutions at this time. Although I think, an apology would have been in order.

To be completely fair and unbiased, I must emphasize the great care and attention my wife received in the ICU. The nurses were truly "Angels of Mercy," they spared no effort to sustain the return my loved one to me.

The nurse who attended her in the Main Hospital, especially the Asian nurse, on the Saturday and Sunday, who also performed the duties, for which they are renown.

I had interviews with the Hospital Administrator, the Director of Nursing, and the Head Nurse on duty for that particular shift. I was promised I would get a full investigation. To the best of my knowledge, the nurse concerned, was not even reprimanded, or even interviewed. If she were, I was never informed.

Efforts to solicit the aid of Lawyers brought only sympathy. Their fee's to even start an investigation were beyond my means. With the solicitors help, and my limited resources, I did manage to obtain the files for those last two weeks.

These provided me with ample examples of incorrect times, statements and other improprieties. *"The closing of the ranks, I think they call it!"*

Talk show hosts I contacted with a view of exposure in the Victoria, Vancouver area, they gave me more sympathy, but no opportunity to come out with my story. I offered them my files for their perusal to satisfy any fears of litigation that they might receive. Recent horror stories like mine, have begun to come out in the media

I have just begun my period of mourning, and I have also just finished editing the previous chapters. What comes through clearly is, that I did enjoy my 52 years of marriage, but something else also became clear to me, I had been living in "Denial."

Early in this narrative I made a short mention of the word fault, indeed she did have a fault. I had mentioned it early on, that my wife had once had an affair behind my back. It was commonly thought then, that:

"If they would do it once, they would do it again," much like wives with abusive husbands have to put up with.

As you have read, I had long periods of time when I was away from home, which could allow infidelity to happen very easily of course. There had been little chance of me just dropping in unexpectedly. Did I know this happened? Yes, once for certain, did I suspect it? of course I did.

When I first met my wife, my first impression of her was, that she did not have a blemish on her character. She was always dressed impeccably, and gave off an impression, at least to me, that she was a virgin. I was to find out later, that this was not the case.

Soon after our marriage, she confided to me of several stories of previous encounters, while she had been in the military service, with the Royal Air Force. I had no argument with this, as certainly I was not a virgin myself.

I did not mention in my book, that I had been married previously, actually I only had three weeks of marriage, before being shipped out to the Middle East, for two years. That period of my life ended with a divorce, as on my return to England I discovered that my wife had been unfaithful to me, fraternizing with the Yanks. So, after a period of three years, I divorced her, using her infidelity as my reason.

Following the betrayal by my second wife, who was my best friend, there was a quiet time between us. She had promised me it would never happen again, and life between us gradually went back to normal. Whenever I was away on duty, Iris wrote to me almost every day. I must be truthful though; I had tried to put her affair behind me.

However, all through my marriage I was plagued with recurrent dreams of her having affairs, which she always put down to be just dreams. On one occasion my dream was so real, I did not speak to her until after lunch, I had recognized the face!

I have only disclosed this information to one person, and, as we closed off our confidential talk on that day, she asked me:

"If you were to meet her in heaven, would you forgive her?"

My reply to her, after some considerable thought, was:

"Yes, of course I would"

What you don't know won't hurt you, and I never knew for certain. While we were in each other's company, everything was good. I had a very interesting life, and I was devastated when our life together ended.

She was a good housekeeper, an excellent cook, and a great companion. I have no regrets.

Epilogue

My biography was intended to help others in countering the grief associated with the passing of a loved one. I have discovered that Grief is a many headed serpent. There are so many ways to approach it. No single person can walk in another person's shoes. You must shed the guilt complex all survivors feel, and proceed on with your life.

I had the help of many good friends, you have to circulate, never withdraw into yourself, make new friends, take up a hobby, serve the community, keep active. If another partner turns out to be the way for you to heal, do not feel that you are betraying your loved one.

You will be truly amazed how many of your real friends will accept this departure. Life is for the living, having been there, done that, I can sympathise wholeheartedly with my fellow travellers.

I found it most helpful to talk and write about my loved one, and our life together, regardless of the pain it arouses in me. With the passing of time this discomfort diminishes gradually, little by little, it is replaced by an understanding and acceptance that life is an ongoing event.

The memories of my wife will be with me for ever, I feel that she is with me wherever, or whatever, is ahead of me in life. I have the faith that she would understand.

Lightning Source UK Ltd.
Milton Keynes UK
UKHW040123200620
365293UK00003B/40/J

9 781728 361444